# Change Your Life with CBT

D1462837

# Prentice Hall LIFE

If life is what you make it, then making it better starts here.

What we learn today can change our lives tomorrow. It can change our goals or change our minds; open up new opportunities or simply inspire us to make a difference. That's why we have created a new breed of books that do more to help you make more of *your* life.

Whether you want more confidence or less stress, a new skill or a different perspective, we've designed *Prentice Hall Life* books to help you to make a change for the better. Together with our authors we share a commitment to bring you the brightest ideas and best ways to manage your life, work and wealth.

In these pages we hope you'll find the ideas you need for the life *you* want. Go on, help yourself.

*It's what you make it*

* * *

# Change Your Life with CBT

## How Cognitive Behavioural Therapy can transform your life

**CORINNE SWEET**

**Prentice Hall Life**
is an imprint of

Harlow, England • London • New York • Boston • San Francisco • Toronto • Sydney • Singapore • Hong Kong
Tokyo • Seoul • Taipei • New Delhi • Cape Town • Madrid • Mexico City • Amsterdam • Munich • Paris • Milan

PEARSON EDUCATION LIMITED
Edinburgh Gate
Harlow CM20 2JE
Tel: +44 (0)1279 623623
Fax: +44 (0)1279 431059
Website: www.pearsoned.co.uk

First published in Great Britain in 2010

© Pearson Education Limited 2010

The right of Corinne Sweet to be identified as author of this work has been asserted
by her in accordance with the Copyright, Designs and Patents Act 1988.

Pearson Education is not responsible for the content of third party internet sites.

ISBN: 978-0-273-73715-5

British Library Cataloguing-in-Publication Data
A catalogue record for this book is available from the British Library

Library of Congress Cataloging-in-Publication Data
Sweet, Corinne.
   Change your life with CBT : how cognitive behavioural therapy can transform
your life / Corinne Sweet.
       p. cm.
   ISBN 978-0-273-73715-5 (pbk.)
   1. Cognitive therapy--Popular works. 2. Change (Psychology) I. Title.
   RC489. C63S94 2011
   616. 89'1425--dc22
                                                                    2010033830

10 9 8 7 6 5 4 3 2 1
14 13 12 11 10

Typeset in 9.5 Iowan Old Style by 30
Printed and bound in Great Britain by Henry Ling Ltd., at the Dorset Press, Dorchester,
Dorset

# Contents

# Part 2 How to use CBT to make your life better

# Acknowledgements

Heartfelt thanks to Elie Williams, Caroline Jordan, Rachael Stock, Helen Savill, Jacqueline Twyman and all the other staff at Pearson who worked hard on this book; and to my wonderful agent, Jane Graham Maw, for her usual encouragement and support. Thanks too to Navid Nabijou for his excellent assistance, research and technical drawings and to Clara Potter-Sweet for her sparky design input. Thanks also to Professor Stephen Palmer for his clarity about all matters CBTish, and to Glen Macklin for his experienced insights. Last, but not least, thanks to my fantastic family and friends, especially Rufus and Clara, and Corinne Hughes for putting up with my book production mode, which means lots of tea and TLC. Finally, thanks to Mackerel and Capuccino for all those late night cuddles while writing.

## Dedication

To Cathy Itzin, who inspired me to write, and who really made things change for the better.

## Publisher's Acknowledgements

*We are grateful to the following for permission to reproduce copyright material:*

**Text**

Extract on pages 180–1 © 2010 Mind, adapted from *Understanding Depression* with the permission of Mind (National Association for Mental Health) www.mind.org.uk.

**Picture Credits**

The publisher would like to thank the following for their kind permission to reproduce their photographs:

Pages 58 and 70, KPT Power Photos.

All other images © Pearson Education

In some instances we have been unable to trace the owners of copyright material, and we would appreciate any information that would enable us to do so.

# Part 1

# Understanding the CBT viewpoint

**Chapter**

# 1

'Life is what it is, you cannot change it,
but you can change yourself'

**Hazrat Inayat Khan**

# How can I change my life with CBT?

Would you like to change something about your life? If so, the good news is that you can – from this moment on. No matter how comfortable you might be with things in your life, there's always something you can do that will make you feel happier and more effective. And if the idea of change is daunting, don't worry – this is the book to show you the way, with the help of some scientifically proven techniques, and lots of real-life examples to show you how you too can benefit.

You may well have picked up this book because you feel disgruntled or dissatisfied that you always seem to come up against the same kinds of obstacles in your life. You may even have a sense that those obstacles have something to do with how you operate in the world. If so, take heart. You've taken the first important step towards changing things for the better.

This could be the first time you've decided to tackle your situation, or perhaps you've already tried to change things in your life, using therapy, coaching, common sense or will-power, but may have come to a point where you feel you need something different, something better, or a whole fresh approach, to try to get on top of whatever is dogging your progress, happiness and success. You might even know, deep down, that you are struggling with something specific, or you have 'low' days, panics or obsessions, which are holding you back. Or it could be that you are just searching for something to push you that extra mile, or straighten out some emotional or behavioural kinks in your life.

We can often feel as if everything is all right for other people, while we struggle away with the same old niggling difficulties in private. It's the perennial grass-is-greener syndrome. From the outside I can seem a very confident, outgoing, successful person, and people often say to me *'oh, you wouldn't understand how difficult it is for me, or how anxious I am – it's all right for you.'* Well, actually I do. I've had to tackle my own issues around anxiety, fear, trauma, addiction, death, depression, in fact all sorts of normal human things that are hidden from obvious view.

The truth is, most of us are dealing with something that others don't really know about. Many, many people struggle with procrastination, chronically put things off – clearing out clutter, asking someone out, or applying for a new job – until it's almost too late. Lots of people avoid situations or things that either scare them or limit their lives and choices, through fear, isolation or low self-esteem (whether they know it or not). You're not alone. And this book is going to hold a hand out to you to help you move forward out of any stuck place you might be in.

Having been a psychologist and counsellor for many years I have long experience of many different kinds of therapy and counselling. When I trained in cognitive behavioural therapy (CBT), and learned the techniques in this book, I have to say it was the icing on the emotional cake for me. It turned out that I learned a great deal from my own CBT training. I now practise CBT with myself and others and have found it amazingly helpful because it has opened my eyes to new ways of thinking, behaving and feeling. I am sure it will do the same for you too.

## Time for change

I absolutely believe that change is possible. And desirable. I have experienced it myself and I have seen many clients change before my eyes over nearly 30 years of private practice. In fact the one thing that you can rely on in life is that everything changes. All the time. However, many of us can feel at the mercy of change, or might feel – Canute-like – that we want to hold change back. Well, this book is going to ask you to look forward to change, to welcome it with open arms. And, more importantly, to be in charge of it. For yourself.

What's more, I'm going to ask you to climb into the change driving seat. Quite often people are wary of going to counsellors, psychologists or therapists, fearing they will be 'analysed' or shredded emotionally in some way. This book is not about you being 'done to', it's about you 'doing'. By picking it up, and continuing to read, I am hoping to engage you in a truly life-changing process. It will take a bit of time, and it will need you to decide to go with the flow, rather than resist, but with a bit of effort you should come away with new tools, and a new perspective for changing your life.

**"**The greatest discovery of my generation is that human beings can alter their lives by altering their attitudes of mind.**"**

**William James**

However, there is a more fundamental question to answer. Ask yourself **RIGHT NOW:** *'Do I really want to change?'*

## The change paradox

Through my own clinical, and personal, experience, I have seen many people (including myself, I have to admit) grapple with the thorny issue of change. Many people say, *'I want to change my life'*,

but when it comes down to it – **if it means something actually has to change** – they're not so sure. I have heard *'I want to change, just as long as it doesn't mean things really have to change'*, many times, not always in those words, but whatever the words, it often boils down to what I call 'the change paradox'.

We are usually comfortable and secure when things remain more or less the same, and we often deliberately seek to keep things ticking over, in the same old familiar way as they always have done. We convince ourselves that we like the way things are. You can get comfort from going to your favourite restaurant, and always ordering the same dish; or getting up in the morning, and following the same routine; or keeping the same systems going at work; or going on holiday to the same resort each year. Routine can bring a sense of security, rhythm and calm.

But too much routine can be rigid and deadening and can stop you from being able to grow or 'think outside the box', as the saying goes. Fear is really what keeps us static – fear of the unknown, fear of failing (or, more often, of succeeding), fear of humiliation or rejection, fear of being envied if we succeed brilliantly, and even fear of fear itself.

Maybe some of our resistance to change is linked to what we believe we will have to go through to get there. Many forms of therapy are about learning to dig deep into your distant past, and about reliving pain, and analysing yourself in great detail, and that can be quite off-putting to many people.

**However, CBT is about dealing with the present**. There's no delving into your past, no agonising about what has been. CBT is all about understanding what's going on in the here and now, and taking action to correct anything that is holding you back, or causing you pain.

So can this book really help you? Let's find out.

## Change checker

**How's your life right now?**

Stop for a second before reading any further. Ask yourself the following questions, right now. Tick any to which you answer 'yes'.

**Tick**

1. Are you getting the most out of your life?
2. Is your potential being totally fulfilled? Are you being stretched to the limit?
3. Are you overloaded, pushed too far, stressed out by chaos at home and in the world, and it all seems too much?
4. Do you get into any repetitive struggles with people – or yourself?
5. Do you find yourself repeating any destructive behaviours?
6. Are you stuck in a dead-end job or relationship?
7. Are you wondering about 'going it alone', but feel too scared, in either sphere?
8. Do you blame others for holding you back, or blame life for not giving you the best opportunities?
9. Are you stuck in the past, full of painful regret?
10. Do you beat yourself up, emotionally, or even abuse your body, physically?
11. Have you set some goals, but have yet to reach them, having become somewhat discouraged?
12. Are you finding it hard to deal with the things life is throwing at you, such as the credit crunch, marital breakdown or work pressures?
13. Has life has got tougher along the way than you ever imagined possible?

Tick

14. Are you struggling with addictive habits, such as smoking, or drinking, getting angry, spending too much?

15. Do you feel hopeless about ever being able to give up?

16. Do you have the urge to be 'perfect'?

17. Do you need to check things all the time or wash your hands to reassure yourself constantly?

18. Are you your own worst critic, always judging yourself harshly?

19. Are you intolerant and irritable about other people's foibles and mistakes?

20. Would you like to feel less anxious and more confident?

If your answer is 'Yes' to some (say at least four) of the above, then this book may well be of great help if you really want to change.

# Why CBT?

You might well have picked up this book with some sketchy idea about what CBT is, or perhaps you know someone who has benefited from it. It is a well-respected therapy worldwide, with a proven track record. CBT is particularly known for getting fairly quick and measurable results.

# Introducing Mr Beck

The main founder of CBT, Aaron T. Beck, was a traditional Freudian psychoanalyst who noticed that his clients often offered up thoughts connected to what they feared he was thinking about them. These thoughts ran alongside any other thoughts they might be having about their deeper problems.

Beck called this psychological process 'turning on the intercom' in his seminal book, *Cognitive Therapy of Depression* (The Guilford Press, New York, 1979), when his clients gave voice to the random thoughts that popped into their heads during the session.

## 'Second stream' of thoughts

The client might be talking ostensibly about a particular problem, like their fear of dying, but meanwhile they were thinking here and now things about Beck, such as:

- *'Does he like me?'*
- *'Bet he thinks I'm a bad person.'*
- *'Am I getting this right?'*
- *'Will this work? Is it value for money?'*
- *'This is a waste of time ... he probably hates me.'*

The 'intercom' showed the 'second stream' of thoughts that Beck believed actually revealed 'unhealthy' thinking habits. The 'second stream' showed how unsure, anxious or uncomfortable the clients really felt. Instead of ignoring these thoughts as being irrelevant to the session, Beck began to focus on them as the real starting point for helping someone sort themselves out. His goal was to change the way they thought, in order to change their feelings and their behaviour. (We'll come back to this in more detail in the following chapters.)

However, you might well be wondering, *'Can it work for me? What exactly is it? How do I go about doing it?'* All these questions will be answered in this book, with a clear, step-by-step approach. In a way, it will be like you having come to see me, as your therapist, and me asking you, once you've got comfy in your chair opposite me: *'So, how can I help you?'* or *'What is it exactly you need a hand with?'*

**What CBT is particularly good for, is helping you sort out:**

- **anxiety,** fear, procrastination, shyness – all those awkward things that hold us back every day in our daily lives;
- **depression,** the blues, feeling low, wanting to hide away – and everything else like that;

- **isolation**, avoiding people and things, not wanting to communicate or relate;
- **obsessions and phobias** – anything from compulsively washing your hands or drinking too much alcohol to hating creepy-crawlies, or fearing dogs;
- **low self-esteem, lack of confidence** – all the things you might think, do or feel that put you down, or hold you back.

**❝The greatest griefs in life are those we cause ourselves.❞**
Sophocles

**What this book offers:**

- clear, concise information about how to change if you want to – how to apply tried-and-tested CBT methods to your life;
- straightforward guidance on how to make vital changes, one small step at a time;
- practical advice for keeping on track;
- a real promise that if you use what's in this book properly you could make your whole life better.

**What this book doesn't offer:**

- 'magic' answers or simple 'miracle cures';
- instant fixes or simple answers without your involvement;
- a promise of overnight success without you having to do anything to get it – *you will have to make a commitment to change*.

# How does CBT work?

CBT is a psychological and behavioural approach to change based on scientific principles that research has shown to be effective for a wide range of problems. It has been evolving since the 1950s and has a well-established high success rate, if applied properly and routinely. There are many clinical tests by psychologists worldwide that show you can get dramatic, life-changing results with CBT, although they will take some effort, determination and commitment on your part to achieve.

CBT helps people clearly identify their **core issues**, particularly repetitive, **negative thoughts** (of which they might be completely unaware), in order to think, act and behave differently. CBT has found popularity in an even wider group of people, those who want to improve their lives generally, removing limiting behaviour.

Broadly speaking, CBT believes there is an **ABC** of analysing your problems:

- **A** = an **ACTIVATING** event – otherwise known as a 'trigger'. This might be an *external* event, such as a car crash or a fight, or divorce or an injury; or it might be an *internal* event, like a dream, a fantasy or even a memory, a hormonal change, or even anticipation of something about to occur.
- **B** = your **BELIEFS** – this includes your morals, views, personal rules and ideas; *meanings* that you attach to the external and internal events in yourself, other people and the world.
- **C** = the **CONSEQUENCES** – this includes your *feelings, behaviours, thoughts,* physical experiences, which accompany your emotions.

CBT gets you to differentiate between your *thoughts, feelings* and *behaviours.* For instance, using the ABC technique, let's look at how you might feel anxious about going out to a party on your own. The ABC of this problem might look like this:

- **A** = you imagine going to the party or you remember how you felt walking into a party on your own in the past;
- **B** = your belief might be *'I've got to go to the party alone, otherwise I'm totally useless – how weak is that! If I don't go I'm a failure.'*
- **C** = just thinking about walking into the room alone, all eyes on you, makes your knees shake, your mouth go dry (emotions and physical sensations connected to fear), and you know you'd go straight to knocking back a couple of glasses of wine to quell your nerves or you'd rush out to the loo and

hide, or stand in a corner, swigging a beer, wanting to disappear under the floorboards (behaviour).

### 'Safety behaviours'

Central to the thinking of CBT is to look at what we do to keep ourselves 'safe', as it is often a way of avoiding difficult feelings. So in the example above, we might avoid going to the party altogether to stop ourselves feeling fear, shyness, anxiety. More importantly, CBT takes on the challenge of proving that it is possible to do the very thing you are afraid of once you learn some very simple techniques. Quite often, we are held back more by our fear of what we think will happen than the actual experience of doing the thing we are scared of. CBT sets out to change your behaviour, and your feelings, by teaching you it's possible to do things differently, and feel and behave differently, as a consequence.

## CBT: the popular therapy

CBT has become a very popular therapy. Precisely because it is so 'common sense', can be learned relatively easily, and can get visible results. It's less daunting than some of the more traditional therapies, and can start working straight away. CBT is based on learning and experiencing change, so it's not based on complex analysis or spending hours dissecting dreams. It is also something that you can learn to do for yourself – hence this book. CBT is about learning new skills, and putting them into practice. It's all about looking at yourself afresh, conducting little experiments, and then learning from what you did, so you can move forward, adapting and changing as you go.

It's also about seeing results, which can be measured, and then learning from those results, so you can move on. The results can be tested, and retested, so that you can see that something has really changed or happened. This is one of the reasons CBT has become so popular, and is used in the NHS by doctors, psychologists and many other therapists and practitioners today.

### Specific conditions CBT treats

CBT is also used as a treatment for specific conditions, and for these the scientific evidence shows it to be effective for:

- depression
- anxiety
- panic disorder
- post-traumatic stress disorder (PTSD)
- anger
- social phobia
- chronic pain
- obsessive compulsive disorder (OCD)
- bulimia nervosa
- schizophrenia
- childhood disorders.

This makes it very different from other methods of therapy that tend to involve much analysis of past events.

## Ideas at the heart of CBT: a taster

- **C** = COGNITIVE = it's our *interpretations* of events in life – not the events themselves – that are central.
- **B** = BEHAVIOURAL = *what we do*, how we react to events, impacts on our thoughts and feelings.
- **T** = THERAPY = we can create 'experiments' to test our 'theories' about our thinking and behaviour. We learn from the results, and then retest them again – that's how we change.

## Can CBT work for me?

CBT can be learned with a therapist, in a group, or through a self-help medium, such as this book. There is an emphasis on you doing a lot of the practice work between sessions, which is called 'homework' (but don't let the word put you off). It's essential to keep the CBT process going away from a session or a class (a bit like practising yoga or doing push-ups away from the gym) – so 'homework' is the necessary name of the game. But as with those other activities, you'll see the benefit over time if you keep at it. So, using this book, you will need to decide to keep your 'homework' going in between reading chapters, or dipping in and out. You could decide to do it for a week, or two, or a month – and you will need to stick at doing it to see some benefit.

Of course, the starting point is always with you, yourself, deciding that something needs to change. You need to be ready and willing to look *honestly and openly* at your thoughts and behaviours, and be ready to break old habits, no matter how comfortable they may seem. You may be more than willing to change because you've become fed up with how things are, right now.

> ### Insight
>
> Think back to any time in your life when you have learned a skill. It might be riding a bike, swimming, riding a horse, cooking an omelette, turning a lathe, painting a door, playing sport, making a fire, knitting a scarf, learning a musical instrument, building a wall, planting some seeds, learning a new language. Whatever you did, it took time, effort, you made mistakes, felt frustrated, you failed again, and then, after practice, made more mistakes, until you eventually succeeded. This is how you have probably learned any new skill – with a growing sense of self-worth at finally achieving a result. It's called the 'adult learning curve'.

This kind of learning curve will happen when you try to learn CBT skills. It's just the same as learning anything else in your life. So you will need to:

- identify things that you want to change;
- follow the parts of the book that help you work out how to change;

- then apply the exercises to your life to change both your thinking and your behaviour;

- monitor the changes, adjust, recommit to change, and so on.

**If you stick with CBT, over time, you will begin to change.** You will begin to notice subtle, even profound, differences in how you think, how you act, and there will be a ripple-effect in your life. Don't forget that slight changes in one place will bring about significant changes in every sphere of your life. It's a bit like the 'butterfly effect' from 'chaos theory', whereby small differences at the beginning of something, like the beat of a butterfly's wing somewhere in the universe, will bring about big, far-reaching changes in varying ways, in all sorts of places, over time, somewhere else in space. That's a bit how CBT works: an infinitesimal shift can bring about enormous results – eventually.

## What would you really like to change?

In order to use CBT effectively for yourself you will need to think specifically about what you would like to change. You might not be used to thinking about your life in this kind of ordered way, or it might feel a bit strange to make a 'shopping list' about yourself. It's a really useful exercise and it gives you a place to start from – so have a go. Set aside a bit of time, and do it in private, if possible.

Try to be as honest and as clear as you can be about the things that you really feel are stuck. It might seem they are already part of you, like breaking into a sweat when you have to give a talk at work, or opening the fridge to find something to nibble on, when you're bored. You might feel ashamed about owning up to something, like drinking too much alcohol or having violent thoughts towards other people. Don't censor yourself. The following exercise is about you, and is for your own eyes only. It's to help you pinpoint the things that are really bugging you, and that you'd like to get a handle on.

## Test yourself

**Put yourself under the microscope**

Read the first question below, and then close your eyes for a moment and tune in with your feelings. Wait for a second and then write your answer in the slot below. Try to be as honest as you can be with yourself. Then move on to the next question and repeat the process.

What would you really like to change ...

... About yourself?

| Short term | Mid term | Long term |
| --- | --- | --- |

1. _____

2. _____

3. _____

... About your work?

1. _____

2. _____

3. _____

... About your relationship/partnership?

1. _____

2. _____

3. _____

... About your home life/family life?

1. _____

2. _____

3. _____

... About your physical self/ body image?

1. _____

2. _____

3. _____

... About your health and well-being?

1. _____

2. _____

3. _____

Notice your answers carefully: this is your starting point.

## Setting goals

Now you've identified what it is you want to change, you need to set yourself some goals. Your goals could be very specific or be broad goals, such as increased success and reward at work, being more sociable, having more satisfying relationships, not being a slave to habit. Or maybe just being happy and content. They might even be about living addiction free, being able to handle and enjoy life as it comes or even about deciding to have children. It would be great to feel in charge of your actions, decisions and reactions, rather than feeling overwhelmed by their complexity and variety.

Practical and specific goals could include things such as being able to enter enclosed spaces, like lifts and tunnels, or travelling on an aeroplane. Or your goals might focus on ending negative reactions or obsessions and generally being more positive and less afraid to take on challenge. It might also be that you are 'phobic' about something, say touching spiders, speaking in public or being in open spaces. So your goals may usefully focus on combating your phobias.

**"**One must have chaos in oneself in order to give birth to a dancing star.**"**
Friedrich Nietzsche

## Choose your priorities

Look at where your priorities lie, where the gaps are. Are there any short-term goals which you have been saying to yourself, for some time, that you'd really like to achieve? Do any of the goals seem truly impossible, or unattainable? Notice which areas seem the most urgent to you, and highlight them, scribble on the page, or keep a note in a computer file or diary/notebook. You can come back to this throughout the book and check your progress as you make decisions, and work towards your goals.

## Goal setting for change

A key part of the CBT approach is to:

- identify your problems
- estimate their difficulty
- work our their effect on you

and then

- set goals to challenge them effectively.

**Here's an example.**

Your partner comes home from work after a long day. They slam the front door, stomp up the hall, throw their briefcase down and head for the fridge, looking sulky and not saying 'Hello'. You are in the kitchen, cooking, hoping for a 'Hello' and kiss after your tough day working, but your partner is definitely not making any eye contact – worse, they look like thunder.

You could think:

Reaction 1: *'Oh, what have I done now? I've really angered them. I must have forgotten to pay the bills again.'*

Or you could think:

Reaction 2: *'Someone's come in, deliberately trying to upset me by ignoring me – how thoughtless after the hard day I've had.'*

Or you could even think:

Reaction 3: *'Oh, I see someone's in a bad mood. I'll steer a wide berth and get on with what I'm doing. I'll find out later what's up.'*

Which might you think? In CBT terms, we attach MEANING to external events, and feel EMOTIONS as a consequence. Here, the bad-tempered, sulky partner, fed up after a bad day – is just that. It's their problem.

## Understanding MEANINGS

Typically, however, we see MEANING in their mood, particularly if we have a relationship with them. In Reaction 1, you take it personally, feeling guilty (when in fact the bad mood may have nothing to do with you). By feeling guilty, you then experience bad feelings, which will lead you to behave in a certain way (you may end up sulking, arguing, slamming about, too).

In Reaction 2 you are still feeling there is a connection between the other person's sulking and your own bad day – and decide to take some kind of revenge. This can lead to the 'It's all right for you' scenario, which can end up in a fiery row. However, in Reaction 3 the thought is purely that the bad mood belongs to your partner, themselves, and it may have nothing at all to do with you. You detach emotionally and wait for things to blow over. By not attaching meaning, or reacting to the mood, it allows it to be clear what belongs to whom.

CBT is all about teaching us to tease out the difference between our feelings about a trigger event, and our reactions to it, so we can work out what belongs to us, and what belongs to other people – as in the case of the sulky partner above. Learning to be more rational about our emotions is the name of the CBT game.

# Finally, making the decision to change

If you can see there is a choice about how you react to events and the A, B, C makes sense to you, then perhaps you will find the CBT approach a useful one in your life. Take a moment to answer the questions below that will tell you more about your own attitude to change itself.

---

### Change checker ☑

**Are you willing to change?**

ASK YOURSELF NOW – giving yourself marks out of 10, with 0 = low, 10 = high.

**Are you willing to be honest about your flaws and difficulties?**

0    1    2    3    4    5    6    7    8    9    10

**How self-disciplined are you (when you set your heart on something)?**

0    1    2    3    4    5    6    7    8    9    10

**Are you willing to make the effort?**

0    1    2    3    4    5    6    7    8    9    10

**Can you open your mind to new ways of thinking and behaving?**

0    1    2    3    4    5    6    7    8    9    10

**Do you like solving problems?**

0    1    2    3    4    5    6    7    8    9    10

**Are you prepared to do things, even if they feel strange and uncomfortable, for the sake of change?**

0    1    2    3    4    5    6    7    8    9    10

**Do you find it easy to tune into your feelings?**

0    1    2    3    4    5    6    7    8    9    10

**How difficult did you find this task?**

0    1    2    3    4    5    6    7    8    9    10

---

Look at your answers carefully. Do they show you to be ready, open, willing to change (higher marks), or are you clinging on to your old habits, wary of stepping forwards (lower marks)? You may not be used to being aware of yourself and your thoughts, behaviours and emotions in this way, but actually, the more you practice tuning in and assessing yourself, the easier it will get. Pay attention to the last question – how did you like answering these questions? The CBT approach involves asking yourself many questions and being able to listen to your own answers.

CBT can work for you if you are willing to be absolutely honest and, also, willing and able to face up to feelings and behaviours that might be a bit awkward to face at first. However, the benefits are that once you can see what you are doing, you are in a strong position to start doing something about them.

---

### Test yourself

**Experimental subject number one: YOU**

CBT is deeply rooted in scientific method, and you will learn to look at yourself coolly, and objectively, under the microscope. This might seem a very strange idea, especially if you feel chaotic feelings or behaviours rule your life, or you are a spiritual or religious person, one who believes in 'fate'. Or maybe you love being a 'free spirit' or 'spontaneous' – except you are not really that happy with what's going on in your life. The CBT approach will help you disentangle your thoughts from your feelings, your actions from your thoughts, as so often these get tangled up, creating problems for ourselves and others in our lives.

As you progress through the book you will learn to conduct little experiments with yourself. This might seem strange at first, but in time it will add to your self-knowledge and self-awareness. As you begin to find you and your life changing, you will see the benefits of tackling things the CBT way.

---

**In a CBT experiment, you:**

- test the truth about your existing beliefs in yourself, others, your environment and the world;
- construct and/or test new beliefs;
- contribute and test a CBT formulation about yourself;
- continually adapt the formulation after further testing;
- also adapt your view of yourself, others, your environment and the world, after the experiment is conducted.

## Reality checks

Using CBT will mean your needing to check out your feelings and to look, coolly, at your own behaviour, time and time again. It's a kind of **reality check,** a means of working out what's going on, what's going awry, and realising how to change it. It may sound a little clinical, but after a while you'll probably find yourself watching yourself, at a slight distance, so you are able to change how you think and even how you behave, rather than rushing headlong into your usual way of reacting and being.

Many years ago I went for a job interview for a post I thought I was really suited for in an organisation I'd been longing to work for. I read the job description, which fitted me perfectly, and applied fairly optimistically. I got an interview, which went well, and I left, thinking, *'Yep, that's in the bag.'* So imagine my surprise when I got the letter turning me down for the job. My first thought was, *'Oh, dear, how did I get it so wrong? I must have done terribly, I'm a total failure.'* I was on the verge of going into a total meltdown and hiding under the duvet for days, when a friend simply said, *'Why don't you ask them what happened?'*

I hadn't even thought that was possible. So I took my courage in both hands, and phoned the human resources people, who told me, very warmly, that I'd done extremely well and was indeed a great candidate and perfect for the job, but in fact the position had been filled from inside the company. At this information I felt a lot better. I realised that I had been on the edge of total self-flagellation and self-blame that would have destroyed my confidence completely. In fact, the knowledge that it was actually an 'inside job' was a 'reality check'. It made me see that things are not always what they seem and once you have all the information, feelings can flow in a completely different direction. From then on, I have always asked a company what their recruitment policy is before even filling in the application form – that way I do not waste time and effort unnecessarily.

## So now the big question: is CBT for you?

By the way, at this point you may be feeling CBT is not for you. If so, that's obviously fine. You may also know by now that you would only feel confident of approaching some of the exercises with a trained practitioner. If so, you can locate a CBT therapist near you by contacting www.babcp.com.

You might even want to make a pact with a friend or partner to work through the book together – if you do, make sure that you do it because you want to, and not *for* the other person. Likewise, try not to get into 'policing' the other person's behaviour – it's up to them whether they complete the book or not. (This is especially important if the other person is your spouse or partner, parent or best friend.)

However, if you think you might well be willing and able to open up to the benefits of CBT because this chapter has shown you that you are willing and open to change ... then do continue reading. Let's now get down to the detailed business of beginning to change your life with CBT.

---

### Your CBT toolkit for life

The idea behind the book is to give you a CBT toolkit, so you can use the tools of the CBT trade to change things when you need to. Each chapter should give you a particular set of tools, insights, tips or information, so you can feel empowered in your everyday life, no matter what you encounter, no matter how you feel.

---

> ### Your CBT toolkit for life
>
> **Tool no. 1: Make and stick with your decision to change.**

> ### Homework
>
> Do you want to have a go at changing what's not working in your life? Make your decision. Take another look at the things you put under the microscope on p. 18 and work out if you need to add anything further. Then prioritise your top choice again – and ask yourself: *'What is the key thing I want to change?'* Write it down clearly. Then, set your timescale for moving on your goals, using this book.

Chapter

2

'The unexamined life is not worth living.'

Plato

# Understanding what makes you tick

Do you know who you are? Do you understand how you think? Have you any idea why you do the things you do? Many of us go through life not really understanding why we get upset when we do, or why we feel certain moods, how we react to things, or what makes us have our up days and down nights. We say, *'That's just me'* or *'I guess I'm just like that'*, without understanding how or what really makes us tick. Learning more about yourself, what triggers your anger, what makes you happy, irritable or sad, what makes you work those extra hours, or reach for the wine bottle when fed up, or line up your pencils in a row when stressed, can be a fascinating journey of self-discovery.

Indeed, CBT is all about getting to know yourself. Not in the style of lying on a couch, analysing your past or your dreams, but more in the sense of learning about yourself, in the here and now, in order to get the most out of yourself and your life. For CBT to work you need to become aware of yourself quite a bit more; you need to be able to 'catch' yourself as you do things, or think things or feel things that lead you to behave in certain ways in certain situations – and sometimes lead you into the same old difficulties. It's all about becoming a bit more conscious and thoughtful about yourself and how you react and interact with yourself, others and the world.

Leila, a 30-year-old mother of three children under 10, explained to me that she always tries hard to please people. *'Whatever I do, I always try to do it 110%'*, said Leila. She came to see me because she was constantly getting ill, was exhausted and felt increasingly depressed.

*'I can't understand what's wrong with me, as I've got everything going for me'*, explained Leila. She said her husband worked hard in his family's garage business, and she was left mainly to manage the house, although she did bookkeeping for the firm, late at night, to save her husband money.

What Leila didn't understand about herself – at that time – was that as well as being a full-time housewife, mother and part-time unpaid bookkeeper, she was also looking after her own elderly parents, running errands for friends, and trying to placate an irascible husband, who was never satisfied. In addition, Leila volunteered to organise the primary school fair, which turned out to be the last straw. She got into an argument with one of the other mothers when she forgot to book the bouncy castle in time, and found herself crying uncontrollably for a whole night. This is what brought her to see me. *'I can't believe I made a mistake like that. I like to do a good job, but I'm running myself ragged, so I end up feeling I don't do anything well any more.'*

Leila was unable to forgive herself for making such a big mistake. It was as if her life depended on her being perfect – all of the time – which is impossible, of course. In fact, after a session or two we began to see that Leila had chronic 'people pleaser' patterns that were driven by guilt and a huge lack of self-worth. Underneath it all, she didn't feel good enough, and was trying to please everyone to show that she was really lovable, worthwhile and efficient.

At root, Leila's 'co-dependent' (people-pleasing) behaviour was being driven by what CBT calls a **'core belief'** of *'I'm worthless'*. (We'll come back to core beliefs in Chapter 3.) However, once we began to uncover this core belief – which surprised Leila – we were able to start helping her shelve some of her enormous, self-imposed responsibilities. Her shoulders, after all, were those of an ordinary woman, not the female Colossus she felt she needed to be to get everyone to love her and to give herself a sense of worth. As a consequence, Leila began to understand what made herself tick. And this understanding in turn helped her to start to improve her life in all kinds of new ways.

# Take a fresh look at yourself

To change your life using CBT, I'll be asking you to take a fresh look at yourself, how you act and how you think, so you can begin to solve your problems for yourself. I'll also be asking you to approach yourself quite coolly and scientifically, so you can examine both your feelings and behaviours to untangle any pickles you are in (or repeatedly get into). This might seem daunting and unfamiliar at first, and you might feel like you'd rather not delve into yourself and your motives too much. However, to get the full benefit from this book, and from what CBT can offer you, I hope you will take a moment to think about what follows.

# The CBT viewpoint

There is a basic tenet in CBT thinking: your **mind** has a lot to do with making you **feel** certain things, and **think** certain things, which lead you to **behave** a certain way. This can become a vicious circle with your **feelings** leading to your **thinking,** and your **thinking** then leading to your **behaviour,** round and round, as in the diagram below.

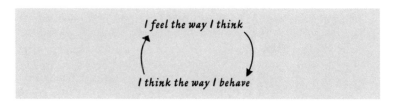

_I feel the way I think_

_I think the way I behave_

❝We do not see things as they are. We see them as we are.❞

**The Talmud**

### How do you see the world?

CBT is all about getting you to re-examine how you see yourself, others and the world. It constantly challenges you to question what you take for granted. Just as Leila saw herself as a people pleaser, and acted accordingly, she could just as equally see herself as 'selfish', and act 'selfishly'. It all comes down to a matter of what we think we believe about ourselves and the world.

For instance, you'll probably be quite familiar with pictures like this one. Take a look for a moment – what do you see?

At first glance you may see the two black faces in profile, facing each other, and then almost immediately you may switch to seeing a white urn shape in the middle. As you continue to look at the picture, your brain will make you switch to seeing first one figure, then the other, backwards and forwards, alternating. It's an uncomfortable, discomfiting experience, but it's also intriguing and tells us a lot about how our mind works.

This picture is called an *'ambiguous figure'* by psychologists, as it confuses our mind's perceptual equipment (eyes, brain, nerves), which is struggling to make sense of what it is seeing. Our brain wants to know: *'Which picture is the "right" picture? Which picture makes sense?'* In fact it's a picture of both things, 'figure' (the black faces) and 'ground' (the white urn). Although your mind is incapable of focusing on both at the same time, it struggles to do so – hence the ***ambiguity***.

**"**The real voyage of discovery consists not in seeking new landscapes but in having new eyes.**"**                    Marcel Proust

In a way, looking at this 'figure/ground' picture, and trying to puzzle out which is the 'right' image, is a bit like trying to understand how CBT makes you see things. In your daily life you may be used to 'seeing' things one way (the black faces), and CBT will come along and make you look at them in a completely new way (the white urn). Essentially, it will be the same picture, it's just that you will be looking at it in a totally different way. CBT will offer you a whole new perspective, so you can try and make sense of things, in yourself and your life, afresh.

## Thinking about your thinking

Have you ever stopped and thought about the way you think? Are you conscious of certain, repetitive thoughts, when you get anxious about something? Or, you might have a tendency to talk to yourself, literally, and tell yourself off in harsh tones? Perhaps you assume people don't like you, or maybe you always think other people are always to blame?

Whatever, the CBT approach to things will mean you will need to learn to think about your thinking: this is called **metacognition** . This might seem daunting at first, but don't worry. Once you begin to see how you think, and pinpoint the kinds of thinking patterns you might have, it can become much easier to work out how and what you want to change.

Take Ben for instance. He's is a 35-year-old carpenter, who is highly perfectionist. His approach to his work is to do a lot of research about what is needed by his customer, then spend ages trying to find the right wood at the right price. That done, he will take a long time to make the piece, whether it's a chest of drawers or some shelves. The problem for Ben is that he has a running commentary in his head that tells him he's getting it all wrong, that he'll do a bad job, and that he'll mess it up.

This makes Ben extra perfectionist and, in fact, can even make him make mistakes. When he does mess up he gets so annoyed that it makes him mess things up all the more. And slow down. Then the job is late and it all goes horribly wrong. Then he loses money and his customers get annoyed at his lateness.

You can see that Ben's perfectionism is actually a handicap, in that it makes him so utterly tense about the whole business that he sabotages himself and his earnings as a consequence. In CBT terms, Ben has a 'thinking error' that is getting in the way of him getting on with the job, and enjoying it. In fact the trap he is falling into, thinking wise, means he is actually slowed down, his work is impaired and he can even ditch a job altogether, lowering his income and success rate. It's a kind of self-sabotage borne out of obsessive perfectionism.

### 'I think, therefore I am'

In CBT terms there are as many ways of looking at the world as there are people. For Ben it's clearly *'I have to do everything perfectly, otherwise I will be harshly judged'*, whereas for someone else it might be *'That'll do, they'll never notice a little mistake'* when it comes to undertaking a task.

For CBT to be effective you need to be able to understand the way in which you interpret the world – so you have to become aware about how you think, what you see, how you interpret everyday events, people, situations. In other words, you need to understand your **cognitions** or your thoughts. It's a bit like, *'I think, therefore I am'*.

## Understanding how your thoughts tick

Most psychologists agree that we 'organise' how we see the world according to our own individual personality, history, experience and beliefs. For instance, when there is an election, if your party wins you might think *'Great, time for a new start'*, but if your party loses, you probably think *'Bah, it's all downhill from here'*. It's the same event, just seen from totally different perspectives (similar to the black and white figure we met earlier).

Thus, our mind 'organises' whatever comes in contact with it to make sense of the world – this is essentially what makes us unique and what makes us tick. In CBT there are six main underlying principles about how we think about things. These are:

1. 'We all interpret the world differently'.
2. 'Changing your behaviour can change your thoughts and emotions'.
3. 'We've all got problems – it's just a matter of degree'.
4. 'Focus on the present to solve the problem'.
5. 'Whole-person approach (Hot Cross Bun Model): "the interacting system"'.
6. 'Weigh up results scientifically'.

## 1. 'We all interpret the world differently'

The word 'cognition' really means our thoughts, beliefs, or, as we saw at the beginning of this chapter, our *interpretations* of what we experience in life (remember the figure/ground picture). Our emotions and our reactions depend on our individual cognitions or how we make sense of what we see.

**PICTURE THIS: a man is facing you, waving his arm wildly on a street corner.**

### How do you *interpret* his action?

- If you are a football fan, and it's match day, you might think he's cheering on his team or other fans (or he might be an enemy fan, threatening you or jeering at you).

- Or he could be drunk, waving his arms around; then again, he could be waving to you because he knows you, or is a family member or old friend, and wants to get your attention.

- Or maybe he wants to pick you up (he fancies you), and is beckoning you over?

- He might be a neighbour wanting to tell you your cat is stuck in a tree.

### Your reactions?

- If you are nervously walking along on your own, and it's getting dark, you might see the waving man, and instantly want to run away, as you feel threatened.

- Or, if you think you recognise him, you might feel overjoyed – perhaps you think he's actually an old friend you haven't seen for ages, and it's time for a reunion.

- However, if you think he's drunk and dangerous, you might cross the road to avoid him.

- Or if you think he's friendly, you might go up to him to see what he wants.

All these possible responses (and more, obviously), are based on how you *interpret* the scene. This is because people react differently to similar events. What we actually see – and understand – is based on our own individual history, our state of mind, our mood at the time, and a whole range of other contextual or environmental factors.

> **"**Life can only be understood backwards; it has to be lived forwards.**"**
> **Søren Kierkegaard**

---

**Insight**

Cognitions lead to emotions

The things above that describe how you might see a man waving on a street corner are *cognitions*. Each cognition gives rise to a different *emotion*: so when we feel the man is a **friendly** football fan, we might feel **joy** or **triumph**; but if we feel he is from the **opposing** team, we might equally feel **anger** or **contempt**. If our cognition is that he is drunk and **dangerous** or a sexual predator, we might feel **fear** and **anxiety**; or if we feel he is a potential **friend**, we may feel **happy** and **excited**. Thus, the first principle of *'We all interpret the world differently'*, means, in CBT terms, *'If people can learn to change their cognitions about things, then they can change the way they feel'*.

---

*Interpreting positive vs. negative events*

It sounds fairly obvious, but it's important to acknowledge here the power that external influences can have on our moods. Positive events can tend to lead to positive emotions; negative events to negative ones. However, because we are all individuals, and we interpret events individually, it's actually possible for us to give events in our everyday lives problematic, or unhealthy, emotional meanings. Sometimes our interpretations can become totally out of proportion and extreme, and we become 'distressed', even 'disturbed', when the event itself does not warrant it.

Take Ivor's late night situation. Ivor came home at around 10.30 on a windy night to find a broken beer bottle in his front garden, near the doorstep, and the hall light on. He'd worked late at the office, but was sure he hadn't left the light on in the morning, when he'd hurried out to work. All of a sudden he was gripped by icy fear. Someone had broken in and burgled his house. It would be a huge, drunken thug, and he'd be lying in wait for him with a baseball bat. He'd read about similar cases in the paper recently. Ivor trembled, dry-mouthed, on the doorstep for a few seconds, unsure of what to do. Should he call the police? He could barely breathe and his knees were shaking. He fumbled in his pocket for his mobile, but couldn't locate it.

Ivor held his breath and listened out for rummaging noises. Nothing. He then slunk sideways and peeked through the front window, but the curtains were drawn. Damn. His heart was going to burst. Ivor could hear the blood rushing in his ears when his front door was suddenly flung wide open and a pretty young woman was standing there, grinning, hands on hips, barefoot. The smell of roast meat wafted by. *'Hi Dad, surprise!'* Ivor nearly fainted with shock at the sight of his daughter, Maie. *'Dinner's ready ... come in. Though it's nearly spoiled now, you're so late.'* Ivor stumbled in after Maie. He'd completely forgotten she was coming home from uni in the holidays and, what's more, she'd made him a nice, welcoming evening meal.

**Ivor's Interpretation of events: his cognitions**

| Event | Emotions | Physical response | Interpretation | Thoughts |
|-------|----------|-------------------|----------------|----------|
| Unexpected light on in house; broken beer bottle in garden | Fear Anxiety Panic Dread | Sweating Shaking Dry mouth Confused thoughts Heart racing | Someone's burgling my house | *'I'm about to be attacked.'* *'I'm being burgled.'* |

## 1. The CBT cognitive model

Once Ivor knew he was safe he could relax, hug Maie, and laugh about his fearful fantasies spurred on by recent newspaper reports. The knowledge that his daughter, not a burglar, was in the house, and that the wind had probably blown the broken bottle into his garden, provided a necessary 'reality check', so he could change his thoughts from apprehension to relaxation, and his behaviour from red alert to relaxation.

Thus, your *behaviour* can change once your *cognition*, or your *interpretation*, of the event changes. Your *emotions* follow *cognitions*, and change accordingly. **So CBT is focused on helping you change your cognitions (thoughts and interpretations), so you can change your emotions, and then also your behaviour.**

Thus,

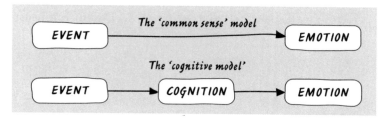

Here's another example of when cognitions (thoughts) can change the emotions surrounding the interpretation of an everyday event.

Dina, 11, is 20 minutes late home from school. She is in her first year of secondary school and has to travel on the bus alone. She has a mobile phone, and usually texts her mother, Joanna, when she is leaving school. Today she has neither texted nor is her phone on when her mother tries to call. Even though it is daytime and light outside, and there is no real reason to believe Dina is unsafe, her mother's heart starts racing, her mouth gets dry and she begins to imagine all sorts of terrible things that might have happened to Dina. By the time the clock ticks round to the hour, Dina's mother has decided her child has been abducted, or is dead under the bus's wheels, or has run away to join the circus. When Joanna finally hears 'Hi, Mum' as Dina comes in breezily, smiling, Joanna is about to explode, either in joy, frustration or relief – or all three. Joanna, like many of us do, has attached unrealistic, exaggerated and powerful emotions to an ordinary daily event, without checking out the reality first. This can lead to an enormous emotional response, and may also lead to a huge behavioural response (shouting at Dina, slamming doors, wailing and gnashing of teeth or sulking – all to Dina's bewilderment and anger).

This is a CBT-style table showing how you can write down what has happened concerning a highly emotional event, such as the above case of Dina's lateness.

**Joanna's cognitive model: fearing for her daughter's safety**

| Event | Emotions | Physical response | Interpretation | Thoughts |
|-------|----------|-------------------|----------------|----------|
| Daughter is late coming home | Fear Anger Panic Grief | Sweating Heart racing Dry mouth Crying Tension | Daughter is in danger | *'I'll never see my daughter again.'* *'I should have made her call me.'* |

Here's an alternative scenario to consider. What if Joanna had told herself *'Don't be silly'* or that *'No news is good news'*, or that Dina was sometimes late because she chatted to friends, or the bus might be delayed (like when there's a gap and then three come at once)?

Joanna could have told herself not to worry, and given herself a whole hour before she did anything rash. Her pulse rate would not have gone up, she could have occupied herself gardening or cleaning. She could have carried out a series of tasks to keep calm, before she had any concrete news to indicate that something might be wrong. Then Joanna's CBT-style chart might have looked like this:

| Event | Emotions | Physical response | Interpretation | Thoughts |
|-------|----------|-------------------|----------------|----------|
| Daughter is late coming home | Curious Relaxed Occupied | Regular heartbeat Calm Rational | Daughter is delayed | *'I'm sure she's fine.'* *'No news is good news.'* |

**Test yourself**

Interpreting your own life events

Can you think of a time when you have misinterpreted an event, so that it seemed more disastrous or frightening than it really was?

● How did you feel once you found out the truth?

● Did it teach you anything about yourself?

Make a note of this wherever you are keeping notes.

Thus, on the one hand your thoughts can change your emotions. Conversely, it's also true that your *behaviour* can change your *thoughts*, and emotions.

## 2. 'Changing your behaviour can change your thoughts and emotions'

Actions speak louder than words, as the old saying goes. Actually, from a CBT viewpoint if you act 'as if' you feel a certain way, it can actually change your thoughts (cognitions). If you change your **thoughts,** your **behaviour** can change, or if you change your **behaviour,** your **thoughts** can change.

This is called the CBT continuum (see diagram below). Either way, you can take charge, and be more powerful, in a situation where you might be experiencing uncomfortable emotions, such as fear, anger, sadness, or a wide range of other negative feelings.

The CBT continuum

### Awesome Audrey

There's a great story about the late Hollywood actress Audrey Hepburn. When she was first invited to a typical Hollywood starlet-packed bash, in the early 1950s, the type of female figure that was popular at the time was the highly curvaceous, all-American, pneumatic, hour-glass shape, sported by beauties including Marilyn Monroe and Rita Hayworth. Audrey Hepburn was a stick thin, shy, gawky, European brunette, and she felt she didn't fit in. She hadn't got a chance of attracting anyone to her (or so she thought). Until she remembered she could act.

Audrey Hepburn recalled the story on radio, later in life, about her decision at one of these excruciating parties to behave like a siren. In her mind she imagined herself as a sexy serpent, slithering along the wall and oozing sensual power. She made eye contact, and lured men to her, mermaid-like. She sighed, pouted, sizzled, and lo and behold, Audrey started shaking up the room. She was soon surrounded by hunks, agents and actors alike. She had used the power of her mind and imagination to exude a strong, sensual power of attraction that actually rose above any physical limitations she might have.

You don't have to be Audrey to try this. A simple thing such as acting 'as if' you were confident at a social gathering can make an incredible difference to how you feel.

Here's another example, from my own life. Over the past 30-odd years I have been on TV and radio as an 'expert' many times. At the beginning of my media career my knees used to shake, I trembled and wobbled, my heart would pound in my ears, and I wouldn't sleep the night before. Then when I was faced with Jeremy Paxman or Kirsty Wark on live TV, well, my voice would dry up to a croak and I would forget my words.

Terrified, I did some confidence-boosting work on myself and decided to walk in just 'as if' I was Kate Adie in fatigues, or Jenni Murray, serene behind the mike. I held my head up (after shaking in the loo for ten minutes), I smiled, I had my three points on a prompt card, firmly held in my trembling paw, and I told myself I had every right to be there. After all, I was being paid to say what I thought.

After the first couple of times (where I still felt nervous, but acted 'as if' I was confident on the outside), I began to relax. So, nowadays, if I am going on *Big Brother* to talk about the housemates' antics, or on the radio to chat about psychological dilemmas, I still feel a twinge of the jitters, but I know this is normal and I tell myself I will be fine and that a little stage fright is manageable and actually makes for a good performance.

## 3. 'We've all got problems – it's just a matter of degree'

One of the strengths of the CBT viewpoint is that it sees emotional problems and mental health issues as part of a *'continuum'*. There is a spectrum of emotion with, say, 'normal/common sense' at one end, and 'severely distressed' or 'exaggerated' at the other. The whole spectrum represents what it is to be a human being, experiencing human emotions. CBT therapists see themselves as being just as human (and fallible) as their clients – so therapy is not about an 'us' and 'them' situation.

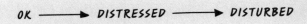

*The spectrum of emotion*

### Do as I do, not as I say

I was working with a regular client, a 16-year-old anorexic girl (let's call her Bea), who had not been out of her house for months. Bea believed that she was enormously fat, too grotesque to be seen in public (whereas she was actually painfully thin). She thought people would stare at and ridicule her for her body size.

As a way of trying to help her, I decided I would go out in a very skimpy dress alongside her on a short, rare outing, and show Bea that it was fine to go out, regardless of my shape or size. However, I was indeed a bit lumpy and bumpy at the time, having recently had a baby, and not without my own feelings of self-consciousness about the shape and size of my own body. I found myself wanting to check myself out in the mirror or windows as we passed shops, thinking, *'Does my bum look big in this?'*

Bea was 'disturbed' in that the level of her 'body dysmorphia' (unrealisitic view of her body, believing it to be huge when it was indeed tiny) was keeping her imprisoned in her home. Whereas I was also somewhat 'distressed' about my body shape, it didn't hold me back from going out, even though I had some preoccupying thoughts about not being svelte or perfect enough. We had the same problem – just in very differing degrees of severity – and impact on our lives.

## 4. 'Focus on the present to solve the problem'

CBT is all about living in the 'here and now'. Traditional psychoanalytic therapies, derived from Freud and others, have tended to delve into the past, to try to pinpoint the root cause of any psychological and emotional difficulties. When the Behaviourists came along in the 1950s, they wanted to short-circuit this way of thinking, finding it too long-winded and inaccurate.

The focus of therapy has became very much about tackling the present moment, including all the emotions and distresses experienced in that moment. CBT theory therefore involves helping the client – you – work out how to handle the present, rather than digging up all the details of the past. If the past comes up, which it may well do, it is noted: but it isn't the focus of the therapy.

Take Dean, 21, an unemployed ex-student, who dropped out of university having got depressed and turned to drugs for a while. He'd found it almost impossible to get up in the morning. He had spent a lot of his life hiding in bed, not facing things, and being late. However, with help from a good friend he kicked the weed, and eventually got to a JobCentre, went on a Learn Direct training scheme, and was doing a certificated IT course.

Finally, he had found something he liked doing, and was good at. He was motivated and was going to sit some exams. However, when I saw him, he was terrified he would oversleep and not get up. Instead of focusing on the past, and all his failures and mistakes, which he kept referring back to, we made a chart of the times he had got up recently.

To Dean's amazement, he realised he was getting up most days at 7.15a.m. and leaving the house at 8.15 to get to his course. In his mind he still believed he was a slob. Somehow his cognition had not caught up with his daily reality. We wrote down a detailed list of Dean's wake-up times over the past month, and Dean soon saw that, in the here and now, from today and this day forward, he had changed a very deep-seated behaviour for the better. He was beginning to succeed, and now he could build on that success.

### 5. 'Whole-person approach (Hot Cross Bun model): "the interacting system"'

The focus in CBT is on the relationship between the person (and their thoughts/cognitions) and their environment – how it affects their emotions, physiology and behaviour. There is a 'Hot Cross Bun' model that CBT therapists use to help you chart how all of these things fit together. It's believed that the Hot Cross Bun model is something that can help you see, for yourself, graphically, how you tick.

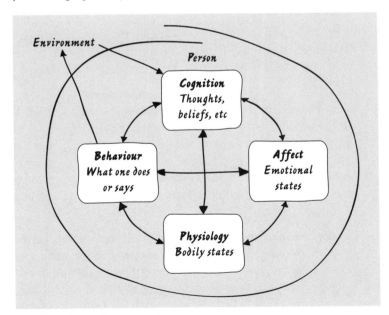

The Hot Cross Bun model

Let's take a real-life situation, and map out a Hot Cross Bun chart.

Sanjeev, 45, has been for a job interview as a taxi driver. He was made redundant recently from a job he had done for nearly 20 years in a components company. He is still upset about it, as he didn't get a proper pay-off. Sanjeev is waiting for a call to say he has got the new job, but he's not very confident. He worries that they may not want to employ him as he's 'too old'.

Thus, his thoughts (cognitions) are typically negative: *'I'll never get a job/no one will employ me now'*. This is affecting his emotional state (affect), so he feels depressed, which is turn is affecting his body (physiology). Sanjeev has had a series of colds recently, and cold sores, and feels lethargic, with a loss of appetite. His mood is low, and he is staying in more (behaviour), especially waiting by the phone for the call to come. He feels the taxi job is a lifeline and his low mood is stopping him from trying all other

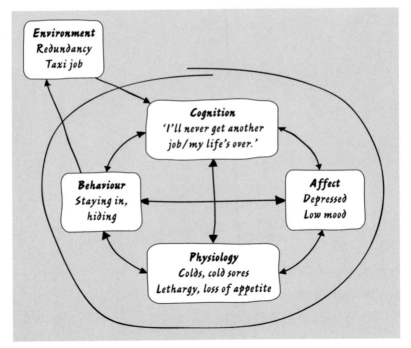

*Sanjeev's Hot Cross Bun model*

avenues, which is probably what he needs to do. But as his confidence is low, he is finding it hard to get the energy and focus to put himself back out there, and follow every lead.

### Make your own Hot Cross Bun model

Take a moment to think about a specific event that has happened in your own life recently. Maybe it was a row with your partner or spouse, or you made a mistake at work, or you wanted to achieve something and failed. What were the cognitions (thoughts), the affect (feelings), the physical reactions (bodily states) and behaviours (actions, reactions) that you had at the time? What was going on in the environment, too, and how did it affect you and the outcome? See if you can write down your own Hot Cross Bun model.

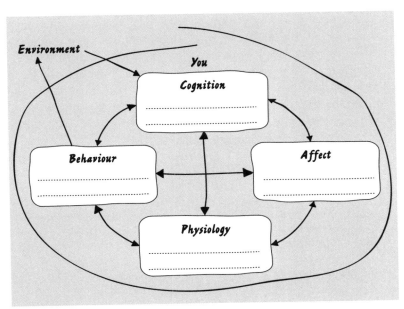

*Your Hot Cross Bun model*

## 6. 'Weigh up results scientically'

There is a focus on *measuring results* in CBT work to show things are really changing. This reflects the fact that CBT has grown out of the more clinical, scientific side of psychology.

### Here's a typical example

Sandra, 50, is terrified of finding a spider in her bath. She usually screams, runs out of the house, and doesn't come back for ages if she finds one there. Sandra's always been scared of spiders. In a CBT session she would be asked to estimate her fear, coolly, on a scale of zero to ten. Sandra says a full ten out of ten, without a doubt, and shudders at the very thought.

Using CBT scientific methods, which involves getting her used to looking at pictures of spiders, even being in the same room as a tiny one, or actually seeing one sit on her therapist's hand, she is then asked to reassess her fear of spiders. This is called 'exposure' to the source of her fear (we will come back to this in more detail in Chapter 7).

Sandra surprises herself by saying seven or eight. Her CBT therapist points out, optimistically, that her fear has come down from an all-out ten, to seven or eight. Quite a significant shift. Together they then work out what she could do next to bring the fear down even lower. It might be she could actually be in the bathroom, with the door open, and with a spider in the bath; or she could even touch a spider on the therapist's hand? In the end, she could even try to let a tiny money spider tickle the palm of her own hand herself?

It might take several sessions to get there, but she would gradually gain confidence from the fact that – from this first session on – she managed to stay in the same room as a tiny spider and not run out screaming. Her confidence would build, as her fear lowered, and her picture of herself as someone terrified of spiders would eventually change.

So far, in this chapter, we've looked briefly at:

1. how we interpret what we experience in the world affects how we feel and behave, and how we feel affects our thoughts and behaviour;

2. how we can map out our difficulties and see them clearly in a Hot Cross Bun model, seeing how everything interacts with itself;

3. how CBT scientifically tests your reactions, helping you adjust as you change.

**"**A pessimist sees the difficulty in every opportunity; and the optimist sees the opportunity in every difficulty.**"**

**Winston Churchill**

# You have your own unique point of view

## Glass half-empty or half-full?

You are the sum of all of your experience in life. Obviously, you will have developed your own point of view, your own theories about the world, your own values and beliefs, your way of interpreting what happens to you from the minute you wake up to the minute you go to sleep (and even while you are asleep, where you have dreams and process your experiences). Your own viewpoint or belief system will be constantly testing your ideas against your experiences, to see if they hold up.

We all know the old philosophical cliché about whether you see a glass half-filled as either half-full or half-empty – depending on your personal viewpoint (basically optimist versus pessimist). For instance, if you get asked out on a date and you say *'Oh I guess s/he was stood up by someone else'* (half-empty), rather than, *'Wow, s/he must really fancy me'* (half-full).

If you are a 'glass half-empty' kind of person, you might think bad things always happen to you, or if something good happens, you'll then be thinking *'Something bad will happen now, I'm sure of it'*. This is classic pessimism, and may well have its roots in your life experience or belief system. Similarly, thinking the glass is 'half-full' means, optimistically, if something is going well, you might think *'Yes, and hopefully better things are to come, bring them on'*.

## Change checker

**Test your own viewpoint**

If you want to use CBT as a way of solving your problems, you will need to become aware of your own particular viewpoint about life. Ask yourself the following questions, aswering 'Yes', 'No' or 'I don't know'.

- Am I a glass half-full kind of person?
- Am I willing to examine my **underlying assumptions** about life, people, events, how the world works?
- Am I willing and able to try out new ways of doing things, and thinking about things, to see if I can change my viewpoint?
- Am I willing to review my beliefs, to examine them carefully, and work out which work, and which don't?
- Am I willing to ditch the ones that are not working in my favour?
- Am I brave enough to look at the way I might even be distorting things that happen to me to hold up my pet beliefs?

Look at your results: check how many 'Yes' and 'No' answers you have. What does this say about your negative or positive viewpoint? Or are you undecided?

# Resistance to change

You might feel it is a matter of personal pride, or a fight to the death, to defend your entrenched principles or beliefs. They may have their roots in religion, or hard-won life experience, but CBT is going to ask you to open your mind, and make yourself open to change, by challenging all the firmly held beliefs, values, ideas that you may have held for years about the kind of person you are, or how the world actually works.

Why? Well, if you want to change, then you will actually have to change your perspective about – first and foremost – how you see other people, the world and yourself in it. To do that, you will need to understand better and focus on what is going on in your mind to lead you to think and act the way you do. This doesn't mean hours of self-analysis ahead, but it does mean becoming aware of yourself, in a practical, realistic way, in order to carry out some very interesting scientific experiments on yourself. This will help, so you can see in more detail what you do, what you think, how you behave and how the three things work together. In other words, it will teach you to understand how you tick.

## Onwards and upwards ...

CBT can provide you with some powerful tools – in your toolkit which you can carry around with you daily – to help combat the half-empty underlying assumptions that may be running your life. If you want to become aware of these assumptions, using CBT as a toolkit to give you insights into yourself and strategies for change, then it will be possible to change yourself using CBT. The first step is to understand more about how you may be thinking, deep down, as you go about your daily life ... and it is to this we now turn.

---

### Your CBT change toolkit

Tool no. 1: Make and stick with your decision to change.

**Tool no. 2: Understanding how you interpret the world and how you 'tick'.**

---

## Homework

### 10-minute exercise

Think about a recent event, or series of events, where you have made snap decisions or quick interpretations about what has been going on. A row with a friend or partner, a difficult meeting at work, a money situation, a tussle with your child. Take one situation and think about whether or not you could have thought about the event differently. Did you have all the facts to hand? Did you jump to conclusions? Were you able to see the other person's viewpoint? Did you feel upset or annoyed or angry before you knew all the facts? Could you have looked at things differently? Jot down two or three situations and allow yourself to think around the problems – could there have been any other interpretation than the one you came to? If so, what? What might you do next time?

Chapter

3

'Most folks are about as happy as they
make up their minds to be.'

Abraham Lincoln

# Noticing your negative thoughts

Your life is in your hands. However, your mind will often be playing tricks on you, so that you don't feel as if it is. You might tell yourself that you want to be successful, happy, competent, loved, productive, organised, calm, positive – but then something is always tripping you up. Something seems to bring you down. Or, somehow things don't quite work out, and you find yourself in the same old pickles with people, deadlines or money.

Maybe you find yourself coming to the same old dead-ends in jobs, relationships or in any other part of your life that really matters to you. Indeed, you might already be very successful, but feel that something is getting in the way of you achieving even more, or that you are only successful in some parts of your life and not others.

As we have already seen in the last two chapters, the CBT viewpoint is that it's actually you who is probably tripping yourself up, bringing yourself down, sabotaging your own success, making yourself fail or holding yourself back. This is down to the prevalence of negative thinking – which you may not even be aware of. Sometimes seemingly positive people are still having negative thoughts, but might simply not be able to see them. They can be like an undercurrent, which surfaces from time to time. Or you might not like to think of yourself as negative, while being a bit too critical or strict, when you're in the mood.

This chapter is going to explain in more detail the way CBT looks at how our own negative **core beliefs** and **underlying assumptions** can set us up for failure, and also make dealing with life's ups and downs all the more difficult to deal with as a consequence.

**"**When one door of happiness closes, another opens; but often we look so long at the closed door that we do not see the one which has been opened for us.**"**
Helen Keller

## Spot negative thinking in everyday life

Take a moment and think about people you know in your life. Is there anyone who gives you an 'up' feeling of energy, enthusiasm, lightness or fun? Then think about the people who give you a heavy feeling, a draggy, down, gloomy sense of doom. I used to go swimming every morning and the attendant always said 'Hello' with a broad smile, which brightened my day and made it a pleasure to meet her. My postman also has a light quip on the doorstep when he drops off the day's post. These people are the 'up' people in life, who meet life's challenges and troubles with a positive, glass half-full perspective. I think they are the ones who are resourceful, resilient and also survive when times get tough.

These kinds of people are so different from the people who are moany or irritable. Or who even shout obscenities out of their car windows the minute the traffic lights turn red. Or those who find the downside in every situation, are very draining and often create their own negative reality: they can be overly critical about everything, push past in a fish and chip shop queue, or even, in extremes, pick fights at bus stops.

These are the people to steer clear of, as their negative energy is often set to explode with the slightest provocation. Personally, I find myself turning round and crossing the road when I see such a person coming – I know their conversation will be peppered with moaning and groaning about the council, or annoyance about the weather.

They always look for the rot in the flower and make hard work of being alive. It's a shame really, as they miss out on a lot that could be good. Do you know anyone like this? Do you give them the time of day, or do you swerve out of the way, too? Or do you, by any chance, even have a sneaking feeling that you can be like this?

**Insight**

**'Can do' mentality**

The lesson from anyone who has overcome their difficulties is that they listen to a little voice inside that says *I can* instead of *I can't*. Positive thoughts prevail over negative ones; determination to succeed and change overcome lethargy and stagnation. It's all a matter of decision, of focusing on goals, of making an effort, of looking to horizons and working towards them. It's the essence of turning the negative into the positive.

## Thinking about your thinking

As we saw in the last chapter, it might seem a bit strange to become so aware of your thinking, and it will take a while to get used to it, but CBT is asking you do just that: start thinking about your thinking. It's what psychologists term 'metacognition'. It might seem very weird to do at first, and people with a scientific leaning (the left-brain dominated among us), tend to find it easier to do than the more artistic (right brained). However, it is possible to start tracking your thinking – and get a sense of what goes through your head if you practise it daily.

Generally speaking, men are slightly better at this task, as they are somewhat conditioned to be a bit more unemotional and distanced about looking at their feelings; while women might find it harder to disentangle their thoughts from their feelings and be objective about their thoughts. On the other hand, women have the advantage of generally being more in tune with their feelings, whereas it's quite a tough task for many men to become aware of their emotions at a micro level. Although these are generalisations, there is probably a strong grain of truth in them.

## Understanding emotions the CBT way

**"Thoughts are opinions not facts."** (CBT motto)

We have already seen that CBT is about identifying negative thoughts which lead to negative feelings which lead to negative emotions, and negative behaviour, and vice versa.

CBT believes there are three main types of 'cognition' or thoughts:

1. Negative automatic thoughts
2. Dysfunctional assumptions and
3. Core beliefs

Imagine a glass of soft drink with froth on the top, liquid in the middle, and sediment at the bottom: that is how the three levels of cognition are organised in the CBT model.

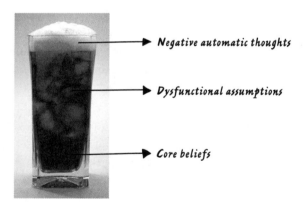

*Negative automatic thoughts*

*Dysfunctional assumptions*

*Core beliefs*

## Negative automatic thoughts

Negative automatic thoughts, which we'll call NATs for short from now on, were first named by the founder of CBT, Aaron T. Beck, and are fundamental to CBT's understanding of how our emotions work. NATs are the kinds of thoughts that flit through your mind all the time. They are thoughts like the 'stream of consciousness' you can read in novels by authors such as Virginia Woolf or James Joyce. They are our brains' background noise.

NATs come and go 'automatically', flit in, flit out, like black bats of doubt and distress, almost unnoticed as we go about our daily lives. You miss the train and think *'Stupid idiot, you're always cutting it too fine'*; or you try on clothes in a shop, look in the mirror and think *'Yuk, you need to lose weight'*. NATs are the constant 'chatter' that pervades our minds 24/7: negative ideas, comments, bad thoughts about yourself. They are the constant put-downs, like a running commentary, that undermine your confidence and self-esteem. They are the 'second stream' of thoughts that Beck noticed (see Chapter 1, page 11).

The first thing CBT believes you need to do is pin down those black bat thoughts, and begin to notice them as they come and go, flitting in and out of your conscious mind. If you look at the diagram of the glass, you can see that NATs are the 'froth' at the top. They are bubbling away, revealing what you are thinking or feeling at any moment in time. They show the meanings we are taking from what is going on around us. They also reveal how we interpret the world, and where we see our place in it. NATS are the surface manifestations of what is bubbling away underneath, much deeper down, at a psychological level.

Miles, 47, a City businessman, grew up with a highly critical father, a military man, who never said *'Well done'* and always picked holes in anything he did. Not surprisingly, as an adult Miles found it very difficult to congratulate himself on anything he achieved. Worse, he wasn't able to accept positive comments from his colleagues, family or friends. He put himself and others down, whenever he could. And, when it came to his own children, he was the harshest taskmaster, finding fault in everything they did or didn't do.

It was only later, when his business failed, and his wife left him – taking the children – that Miles was forced to face the impact of the negative beliefs that he had ingested from childhood. He had a 'breakdown', or rather an emotional and physical collapse, which made him face himself. With help from a CBT therapist he saw that if he wanted to rebuild his life and relationships he was going to have to learn some new ways of 'seeing' himself and others, and put his tendency to rubbish everything in sight on hold. And the place to start with all that was with being less critical of himself.

## NATs seriously erode self-esteem

Part of learning to use CBT to change your life hangs on you making the effort to become aware of your NATs and how they are controlling your life, as in Miles's situation above. NATs are like a constantly nagging commentary, and being negative in nature they will be constantly commenting on you, bringing you down, casting a dark shadow over whatever you try to do or achieve. Tracking your NATS is definitely a good place to start if you want to tackle your deeper, emotional problems. NATs can have a devastating drip, drip effect, wearing down your self-esteem and self-confidence.

The practice of CBT does not want you to analyse your thoughts (unlike other therapies you might have encountered), but it does want you to notice them. Thus, NATs are:

- **there all the time,** chatting away – maybe you just have to start noticing them;
- **conscious** – they reveal what you are thinking, moment to moment (they don't have to be dug out);
- **put-downs** – because they are negative in nature, NATs pull you down, and lower your mood;
- **specific** – to the situation you are in (i.e., walking down a dark street at night – *'I'm scared, I'm going to be attacked'*);
- **believable** – they are the labels we give to ourselves, so we trust them (e.g., *'I'm useless with people'*, *'I'm too fat in jeans'*, *'I'll always miss deadlines'* or *'I'm hopeless at choosing the right partner'*, or *'nobody loves me'*);

- **self-talk** – we can talk ourselves into something, or talk ourselves out of something: we label ourselves and believe the label;

- **chronic** – especially if you are struggling with deep-seated problems in your life, such as depression. Your NATs will constantly be telling you how useless, unlovable, worthless, helpless and isolated you are.

## Regular CBT Thought Records

As NATs reveal your ingrained thinking habits about yourself, others and your experience of the world, you really need to start becoming aware of your NATs as soon as possible, as in the Thought Record exercise on p. 64. To really change your life with CBT you need to keep a daily Thought Record of your NATs regularly over the period of reading this book. Or you could make a decision to follow your thoughts for a day, a week or a month – even just doing it for a few hours can help make you more aware, especially at first.

### Thought Record: losing your wallet

| Event/Situation | NATs | Emotions |
|---|---|---|
| You lose your wallet | *'I'm such a careless idiot.'* *'Why am I always so stupid'?* *'The world's a horrible place.'* | Self-loathing Shame Anger Humiliation Fear Frustration |

From a CBT viewpoint the event of losing your wallet is attributed meaning, and your NATs show how you interpret that event. Obviously there are many other interpretations you could bring to the same event: some people might take losing their wallet in their stride, shrug their shoulders and say, *'Oh well, my wallet was worn out, anyway.'* Others might go into total meltdown, wring their hands and pull out their hair. While others still might coolly make phone calls to the credit card companies and the police. Some might even be pleased, as they can claim on insurance, or escape paying the bill at dinnertime. In other words, the meaning we assign to the event, and the feelings we experience during and afterwards, are down to the thoughts/ cognitions and interpretations we have attached to that event.

This idea is central to grasping CBT and it's worth taking a second to pin down your own NATs about something that's happened recently: maybe you missed the bus, or were late for a meeting; perhaps you got the wrong sandwich order at lunchtime, or you were shouted at by another driver. You could have been annoyed at someone, or felt you couldn't cope with something. Make it a specific incident that brought up negative feelings, then have a go at filling in the chart below.

---

### Test yourself

Identify Your Own NATs

| Event/Situation | NATs | Emotions |
|---|---|---|
|  |  |  |

---

This exercise should help you begin to see how you may be interpreting a typical daily event and attributing your own NATs to it.

---

### Test yourself

Take a second and ask yourself:

- What kind of thinker do you think you are?
- Are you more right or left brained?
- Do you find it hard or easy to think about your thinking?

Make a note of your answers.

---

## Hot thoughts

Once you start thinking about your thinking, you should begin to see some particular, emotionally charged thoughts popping up, over and over. These are called 'hot thoughts' in CBT terms – these are the thoughts which preoccupy you, which are filled with negative emotion, and which disturb you. That's why they are 'hot', in other words, charged with emotion.

When you make your Thought Record, you need to note down the thoughts that are particularly 'hot'. This does not mean 'hot thoughts' about sex necessarily (although that might come into it sometimes), rather they are thoughts which preoccupy you the most, which seem the most loaded with distressed feeling and which recur the most often.

Hot thoughts can be things like:

- 'My life is over ...'
- 'I'll never be a success ...'
- 'Nobody really likes me, and I'll never be popular ...'
- 'I've failed again, typical of me ...'
- 'I can't cope any more, I could murder a pint ...'

*Examples of hot thoughts (typical NATs)*

Typical CBT Thought Record: when you have lost your keys

| Event/situation | Feelings | Automatic thoughts | Case for... | Case against... | Alternative balanced thought | Re-rate feelings |
|---|---|---|---|---|---|---|
| Cannot find keys in house | Anxious 75%<br>Ashamed 40% | 'I may have lost them outside of the house ...'<br><br>'Anybody could pick them up ...'<br><br>'I'm such an idiot for losing them ...' | 'If I thoroughly search the house and can't find them, the chances are that they have been lost outside.'<br><br>'I could have been more careful in handling my keys.' | 'I have misplaced keys many times before, and have always eventually found them in the house.'<br><br>'Even if somebody does find the keys, they have no way of knowing my address.'<br><br>'I can always change the locks.'<br><br>'Keys are small objects which are easy to misplace: it's not completely idiotic to lose them.' | 'The keys may still be in the house. Even if they are not, and have been lost outside, the danger posed to me is minuscule, and I can react accordingly by changing the locks.' | Anxious 30%<br>Ashamed 30% |

## Keeping a Thought Record

Look at the Thought Record opposite about losing your house keys. This is a typical situation that can set off your NATs big time. The feelings such an event can stir up are usually anxiety, fear and shame. Also anger and irritation at being so forgetful. The automatic thoughts might be: *'Anybody could pick them up. ...'* (fear), or *'I'm such an idiot for losing them...'* (anger at self).

If you rate the intensity of your feelings when you have first lost your keys, they might show 75 per cent anxiety (*'If they are outside the house, then someone could find them and break in?'*). But once you have been able to think through the consequences, and have achieved a more balanced perspective (*'The keys may still be in the house'* or *'I can change the locks'*), you may re-rate your anxiety at 30 per cent.

Beck suggested you sit down, at the end of the day, and make a note of your NATs surrounding particular incidents that have occurred during the day. Using a similar grid to the one above, you could keep a note on your mobile, laptop, diary or notebook – wherever you pin down your thoughts – to make them conscious. Just catch them and write them down. Then you can begin to compile a valuable record of the repetitive thoughts that can dog your success or progress in life.

❝When you spend time trying to mend a leaky barrel, you neglect the methods and above all the ways of being that will allow you to find happiness within yourself.❞ Mathieu Ricard

---

### Insight

**Learn to catch your thoughts**

Think of yourself as having a psychological butterfly net where you are going to 'catch' the black bat thoughts as they 'flit' past every few seconds. Like an intrepid Victorian explorer, you want to catch them so you can pin them down, examine them and thereby understand more about them. If you do this you will begin to see what kind of 'species' of preoccupation or distress your thoughts belong to ... giving you insight into yourself and your ongoing, typically human, difficulties.

**Seven excellent benefits of keeping Thought Records:**

1. They show you how your moods change over a day, a week, a month.

2. They reveal any repetitive thinking patterns you might have in everyday life.

3. The very act of writing things down will help you become clearer about how you think.

4. They will show you how preoccupied you are with certain things – so you can start doing something about them.

5. They are a good discipline, and help you look at yourself more objectively.

6. They are a record you can refer back to, so you can see how you have progressed over time once you start using CBT.

7. In time you will be able to work out a more balanced, alternative way of thinking because you trained yourself to look at your thoughts on a regular basis.

# Dysfunctional assumptions

Going back to the glass model earlier in this chapter, the second layer of cognitions that CBT focuses on are dysfunctional assumptions (DAs), which are in the central part (the body of the beer), beneath the bubbling froth of the NATs, and above the heavy sediment of the core beliefs. DAs make up the main body of the pint glass, as negative thoughts bubble upwards to create the accessible froth on top.

**Thus, DAs:**

- may be unconscious thoughts, and not so easily accessible or easy to trace as NATs;

- may be culturally reinforced or defined (such as being a woman who always puts others first; or being a man who must earn enough to support a family/succeed financially; or being a black person and being made to feel like a 'second-class citizen');

- take the form of conditional statements ... *'If I lose my wallet I should be punished by being miserable'; 'If I argue with people and get what I want, I'll be rejected because I'm selfish – so I'd better put others first instead'*;

- are often rigid, narrow, controlling, generalised thoughts that can feed feelings of hopelessness and helplessness;

- actually feed into the NATs, as they are the source of so much unhappiness, preoccupation, anxiety, depression, obsession, or whatever else we may be wrestling with emotionally;

- are 'dysfunctional' in that they do not help you cope effectively and flexibly with whatever life throws at you (you tell yourself that you can't go out to the shops, so you can't go out to the shops even if you need to replenish the fridge, which is pretty essential for life).

Say you think that nobody likes you or wants to spend time with you. You tell yourself, in your dark moments, that you have no friends, you're lonely, and it's always going to be like that. This is a **dysfunctional assumption**. In fact, if you look at your address book or mobile you probably will have a selection of names and numbers of people who have been friends and acquaintances for quite some time. There will probably be people in your address book who actually go back to school days, work life and other experiences. In fact, you have just dismissed them yourself, believing you have no friends.

You could challenge this kind of dysfunctional assumption by:

1. contacting an old school mate, work pal or acquaintance through text, e-mail, snailmail, Facebook, or by simply picking up the telephone;

2. deciding to go to that party, birthday drink or event that you have told yourself nobody wants you to go to – although you've been invited;

3. trying to say *'Yes'* if someone invites you out to something before you listen to the little voice inside that says *'Actually nobody likes me, so I won't go'*.

The good part about challenging your dysfunctional assumptions is that you reduce their power every time you see that they only have a hold over you if you let them.

# Core beliefs

Right at the bottom of the glass lie your sedimentary core beliefs (CBs). These are the ones that go back a very long way, right to your early childhood, and form the emotional and experiential sediment that has accumulated over your lifetime.

**Thus, CBs:**

- are more general than NATs and are about the essence of you as a person (*'I am stupid'*, *'I am always unlucky'*, *'I am totally unlovable'*, *'I'm worthless'*.);

- are unconscious, like DAs, and therefore quite difficult to unveil; mostly CBT focuses on NATs, to begin with at least, as they are the more accessible surface manifestations of what's going on deep-down underneath;

- tend to be more entrenched – you may have quite deep-seated, repetitive, complex problems going back to early life and childhood, in the most extreme cases involving addiction, obsession, abuse, trauma and other 'tougher' issues that you may want to tackle.

Darren, 18, a lifeguard, has a core belief that he is totally unlovable. This partly stems back to his father leaving his mother even before he was born. His mother has brought him up alone, as well as she can, but she has instilled in him that people are not to be trusted, as they tend to abandon you (as his father did).

Unfortunately, Darren has drunk in his mother's bitterness, and finds, when he tries to have relationships with women, that he is fiercely jealous and possessive. *'I'm such a jealous person'*, he admits, *'that I don't believe a word they tell me ... I test them out all the time.'* Not surprisingly, Darren is finding it hard to sustain relationships. He is tending to think it's a problem of finding the 'right' girlfriend, when in fact his inability to trust, his core belief he is totally unlovable and will be abandoned, is getting in the way. His mistrust actually drives his girlfriends away, so it's a typical self-fulfilling prophecy.

Thus, the first step is to get Darren to see who actually has been trustworthy in his life: his mum. And, his best friend at school. So there are at least two people he can say didn't abandon him. In fact, when he thinks about it, many of his girlfriends have stayed, and it's been Darren who has actually pushed them away. So, looking at his own thinking and behaviour is a good place to start challenging his self-destructive core belief of *'nobody loves me or stays'*. In fact, they do. He just hasn't noticed it yet.

## Insight

### Individual spectrum of distress

Sometimes CBs arise from a single incident in life, such as being attacked on the street or left by a partner. This can lead to NATs which tell you *'I am always a victim'* or *'Life's simply not fair'*. Or they can be the accumulated result of a lifetime of hurt and mistreatment. If the latter is true of you, you may want to consider seeing a CBT therapist who can steer you and cheer you through the process of identifying your NATs, DAs and CBs in order to tackle them effectively.

The truth is, the longer or harder you've been hurt, the tougher it might be to get to grips with your difficulties, especially alone. But not impossible. At the same time, if you are motivated to change, it may well be possible to get going with this book, or even get yourself a long way down the road, simply by focusing on your NATs. Keeping a regular Thought Record will begin to peel back the shutters to cast a bright light on what you might have been trying to keep in the shade over the years. The accumulative effect of doing this will begin to bring about subtle, but profound, change.

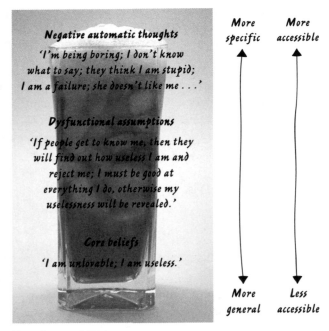

**Negative automatic thoughts**

'I'm being boring; I don't know what to say; they think I am stupid; I am a failure; she doesn't like me . . .'

**Dysfunctional assumptions**

'If people get to know me, then they will find out how useless I am and reject me; I must be good at everything I do, otherwise my uselessness will be revealed.'

**Core beliefs**

'I am unlovable; I am useless.'

| More specific | More accessible | Easier to change |
| --- | --- | --- |
| ↑ | ↑ | ↑ |
| ↓ | ↓ | ↓ |
| More general | Less accessible | Harder to change |

**Spectrum of Distress**

"The journey of a thousand miles begins with a single step."

Lao-Tzu

# The forensic approach to your emotions

CBT has a forensic approach to your emotions. It is not so much interested in the **content** of what you are feeling (as in usual psychoanalytic therapy); it is much more interested in the process of how you come to be feeling or thinking and thus behaving (or vice versa), at any one time. As a consequence, CBT strives to get us to look at our emotions forensically so as to understand them as either **healthy** or **unhealthy**, appropriate or inappropriate.

---

### Reality check

**Healthy vs. unhealthy emotions**

Of course, we're not all heroes like Helen Keller, Nelson Mandela or Stephen Hawking, or whoever you admire, but in our own small ways we can decide to either act on healthy emotions or on unhealthy ones, resulting in very different outcomes in our lives.

**Healthy emotions**

- are negative feelings appropriate to an event – you feel sad when your cat dies;
- lead to constructive behaviours/consequences – you grieve, you plant a flower to remember your cat;
- do not cause difficulties for other areas of your life – you can still function (go to work, see friends) although you're obviously sad.

*Types of healthy emotion*

- sadness, happiness, boredom, remorse, joy, fear, shyness, embarrassment, etc.

**Unhealthy emotions**

- are negative feelings that are over the top for an event – your cat dies and you rant and rave, smash up the house, get hugely drunk;

---

- lead to destructive behaviours/consequences – you punish yourself, punish your friends and family, you don't function (go to work);
- do cause difficulties for other areas of your life – you retreat to bed, stay off work, won't socialise, you drink on your own, because your cat has died.

*Types of unhealthy emotion*

- aggression, jealousy, guilt, fear, depression, shame, envy, isolation, addiction, suicidal urges, etc.

Obviously, feelings are feelings, and no feeling is actually 'bad' in itself. Feelings are a necessary part of our emotional make-up, allowing us to experience the world, feel attached to people, love our children and each other, feel grief over sad events, joy over happy ones, and so on. The issue about healthy or unhealthy emotions, from a CBT viewpoint, is where the emotional response far outweighs the actual event, even to the point of completely distorting its meaning. The reason for this lies in our own individual experience and upbringing, but as CBT is focused on the 'here and now', we need to learn how to be more measured and rational in everyday life. In other words, **CBT teaches us how to be more appropriate and less destructive all round.**

Mandy, 30, a part-time teacher, has worked hard to organise her daughter's eighth birthday party. She likes to think of herself as an organised mother and doesn't like making mistakes (her core belief is *'I'm worthless'*, so she tries hard to disprove this by being extra efficient in life). Mandy has hired a hall, sent out the invitations, bought and prepared the food, and got 20 children running around, playing games with an entertainer.

As she gets to the party she suddenly realises that she has forgotten to make party bags for the children. It's a tradition to give out a little something to say 'thanks for coming' at the end. Mandy is feeling very stressed and humiliated, and starts beating herself up, 'How could I have forgotten the party bags? How stupid am I?' She feels competitive with the other mothers, so doesn't want to admit her mistake.

Mandy is in danger of sabotaging herself emotionally at this point, and flagellating herself fiercely for making a single mistake. Luckily, another mother and good friend notices the problem, and offers to go and buy some packets of sweets to give out at the end of the party. Mandy finds this hard to accept, as she thinks she should be able to do it all, but as she's in the middle of running the party, she has no option.

She has a choice: either continue to think the whole party is ruined by forgetting one thing, or be pragmatic, accept things aren't perfect, and go with making do with an offer from a good friend, despite feeling she should be super-woman. The CBT approach would be to encourage Mandy to be more flexible, and able to react to the situation with a practical solution, say a wholehearted thanks to her friend for her help, and then move on.

**❝**The secret of life is balance, and the absence of balance is life's destruction.**❞**
Hazrat Inayat Khan

## Overreacting

Take another example of Daniel, who has succumbed to flu. He is feeling extremely frustrated about being ill, and fed up with being at home as his work deadlines and unpaid bills are pressing heavily on him. As the day goes on Daniel feels more and more grumpy and disconsolate, so when his wife comes home from work, bringing nice groceries and a noisy toddler with her, fresh from nursery, Daniel sulks.

When his child rushes in to cuddle him, he pushes her off, and she falls over and the shock starts her crying. His wife, disgusted at his behaviour, and despite feeling sorry for him having flu, picks up their crying child and flounces out of the room. Daniel is more depressed and distraught than he was before they came home. He sinks into even deeper gloom, now tinged with self-loathing and disgust.

If we try and understand Daniel's emotional response from a CBT viewpoint, it looks like the table below:

**Daniel's unhealthy emotional meaning CBT worksheet**

| Situation | Personal meaning | Unhealthy emotion |
|---|---|---|
| Pushing his child away | *'I'm a bad dad, I should never hurt my child. I'm a terrible father and husband. I hate myself.'* | Guilt, self-loathing, anger, humiliation, shame |

Daniel's emotional reaction is extreme, and his loss of temper leads him to feel very bad about himself, full of guilt and self-hate. Of course, it's never a good thing to take out bad feelings on a child, but Daniel's guilt is disproportionate to the damage, and also, his shame and humiliation is likely to make him withdraw and sulk all the more – which will hurt the child and his relationship with his wife long term. It would be better if Daniel could separate his behaviour from condemning himself totally as a person, and thus be more healthy emotionally.

**Daniel's healthy emotional meaning CBT worksheet**

| Situation | Personal meaning | Healthy emotion |
|---|---|---|
| Pushing away the child. | *'I wish I hadn't pushed Amy, but I'm sick and stressed. I feel sad and sorry for my actions – but I'm not a totally bad dad or husband.'* | Sadness/ remorse self-esteem |

This second level of emotional response is more appropriate and constructive as what has happened is not the end of the world. Yes, Daniel needs to say a sincere '*Sorry*' to his wife and child, and give hugs and reassurance, but the situation does not need to escalate into one of dramatic, apocryphal, hugely self-critical proportions.

He needs to remind himself and his family of the good times when he's taken Amy to the park, read to her at bedtime, and comforted her when she was scared of the dark. He also needs to recall massaging his wife's back, helping with childcare and succeeding achieving a target at work, so he can begin to get a more accurate perspective. Daniel can look at what happened in this situation more coolly and understand what was going on, then make adjustments so that it doesn't happen again.

---

**Test yourself**

How healthy are your emotions?

Take a moment to look at an incident in your own life. Was there a time recently when you reacted (or overreacted) like Daniel about something? Can you remember an incident at work, with your family, your friends, your partner or children, which sparked you feeling unhealthy emotions disproportionate to the actual situation?

Put yourself under the microscope for a second, and think, honestly:

- What was the situation?
- How did you respond?
- What was the personal meaning?
- What was the emotion?
- Was it healthy or unhealthy?
- Was your reaction appropriate or over the top?

---

"As a man thinks, so does he become. Every man is the son of his own works."

Cervantes

---

## Change checker

This chapter has looked at identifying your:

- **Negative automatic thoughts (NATs)**
- **Dysfunctional assumptions (DAs)**
- **Core beliefs (CBs)**

It has encouraged you to keep

- **A Thought Record**

So you can begin to recognise your NATs.

It's also explained you need to watch out for:

- **Healthy and unhealthy** emotional responses so you can be more appropriate and less destructive.

**What to do with your thought record:**

Once you have written your Thought Record, take a look at it and:

1. Try and spot your NATs.

2. Work out your DAs.

3. Can you identify your CBs?

4. Try and turn your NATs on their head, and say the opposite to yourself as you try to find an alternative reality. So if you think *'I'm ugly'*, think *'I look great'* instead; or if you think *'I'm hopeless ...'* try *'I did quite well. ...'* See how that feels ...

5. Review your Thought Record regularly, looking for any shifts in your thinking.

---

### Your CBT toolkit

Tool no 1: Make and stick with your decision to change.

Tool no 2: Understand how you interpret the world and how you 'tick'.

**Tool no. 3 Notice and note down negative thoughts.**

### Homework

10-minute exercise

Write your Thought Record. Take a moment to think about your thinking. In detail, write down at the end of the day any 'hot thoughts' that recurred during the day. Were they healthy or unhealthy? Did you notice which ones wound you up the most?

Having noticed your negative thoughts, and while keeping your regular Thought Record, we need to move on to understanding your emotions in more detail. In particular, how they can accumulate into what CBT calls your **thinking errors**.

**Chapter**

'Our life is what our thoughts make of it.'

Marcus Aurelius

# Tracking and taming your 'thinking errors'

Remember Eeyore? The gloomy old donkey friend of Winnie the Pooh who lives in the Hundred Acre Wood, with a sign outside his house announcing: **Eeyore's Gloomy Place: Rather Boggy and Sad**? Eeyore's always moaning *'It doesn't matter anyway'* or *'Everything happens to Eeyore'*, in his black-comedic tones. Of course, Eeyore is clearly an exaggerated character – and caricature – but haven't we all met someone like him? Maybe we even recognise a little of ourselves in his deliberate pessimism, where he always sees the glass half-empty, rather than half-full? Naturally, Eeyore's a great foil to the happy old Pooh, living his carefree life having adventures among his dear friends.

Not stretching the analogy too far, the irony of Eeyore is that he literally pulls along his 'little black rain cloud' with him, everywhere he goes, even though he believes that he's actually being stalked by it. While for Pooh, it's anathema to be miserable at all as life is too much fun; for Eeyore, misery is 'second nature', it's just how life is: he's truly convinced himself that misery is his lot.

If were we to examine Eeyore's negative automatic thoughts, (NATs as we saw in Chapter 3), they would probably be something like: *'Nobody likes me anyway'*, and, further down the glass, his dysfunctional assumptions would be *'Everything bad happens to poor to old me'* or *'Nothing ever goes right in my life'*. Finally, we would come to his 'core beliefs, of *'I'm totally unlovable'* and/or *'I'm a total failure'*.

The thing is: it's very obvious to everyone, except Eeyore, (which is why he is so funny), that he is actually hanging on to his negative beliefs himself as they make him feel comfortable.

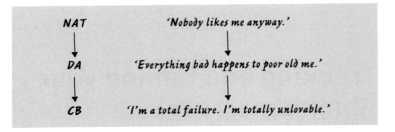

| NAT | *'Nobody likes me anyway.'* |
| DA | *'Everything bad happens to poor old me.'* |
| CB | *'I'm a total failure. I'm totally unlovable.'* |

Eeyore is creating his own reality: being miserable is what he has always known, and what makes him 'Eeyore'.

If we were to ask Eeyore if he wanted to let his 'little black rain cloud' thoughts go, he'd probably say, *'No point'* or *'What difference would it make anyway?'* Eeyore is clinging on to his old, negative way of thinking because it probably feels like the only way he can exist in the world. He might well think, *'Who would I be without my "little black rain cloud" to remind me that everything is bad?'*

## A self-fulfilling prophecy

From a CBT viewpoint, Eeyore is a great example of how negative thinking can totally shape your life – and also how you can keep it shaping your life for yourself. Not only is Eeyore creating his own reality, he's dragging it with him everywhere so that it becomes a 'self-fulfilling prophecy'. If the sun is shining, the sky is blue, it's a lovely day and everyone brings cake for tea, Eeyore will still tug his 'little black rain cloud' along with him, and blot out the sun. *'Then I'll be sorry'* will be his NAT, so he can continue to interpret reality in the same old, pessimistic way.

**"**Life does not consist mainly – or even largely – of facts and happenings. It consists mainly of the storm of thoughts that are forever blowing through one's mind.**"** **Mark Twain**

The CBT approach to Eeyore (if he were to decide he wanted to change, of course), would be to get him to fathom that by living his life according to his negative view of the world (NATs), or pessimistic mindset, it actually works against his own best interests. It's as if the misery button has been pushed in and taped down, so it can never be pulled out again. The challenging part would be to get him to try and see that he is actually doing it to himself, and that he has a **choice** to rip the tape off, and let the button out, so he could take a more optimistic view.

# Identifying 'thinking errors'

The cumulative effect of this kind of negative thinking is that it can chronically control your life, by creating what CBT calls *'thinking errors'*. These are 'cognitive distortions' (see Chapter 3) which have become so entrenched in your personality that you truly believe they are the only way to see things. It's as if Eeyore's 'little black rain cloud' not only covers his head but stretches over his entire life, in all possible directions and as far as the eye can see. The term 'thinking error' is rather like a 'thinking trap', a pit into which negative thinking can pull us, then bury us deep.

Rory, a 52-year-old self-employed businessman, works very hard and feels he doesn't have time to make friends or, rather, maintain his old relationships. His children are grown and gone, and he and his wife have fallen into a dull, routine life. Rory sometimes feels resentful when his wife goes out. She likes salsa dancing, she goes shopping and out to lunch, even dinner, with women friends. Rory, meanwhile, works late regularly and often has supper alone. Over the years Rory has let his old friendships atrophy, he's given up sport, and his contact with his family is now just the odd Christmas card.

Yet Rory firmly believes that other people are the problem. *'I've no longer got any friends'*, he thinks to himself during his down times. Or, *'It's alright for Jane [his wife], she hasn't sacrificed everything for the business'*. In fact, Rory's friends and family have continued to send him birthday cards and presents, in vain. They wish he would get in touch, and don't

> really understand why he doesn't. Also, his old pals still contact him by email or call him from time to time and invite him to the pub. But it's Rory who usually ignores or dismisses them, thinking he hasn't got time for frivolous activities such as socialising. Meanwhile, he sustains his 'thinking error' – that the problem lies solely with other people.

**"The miracle is not to fly in the air, or to walk on the water, but to walk on the earth."**                                        Chinese proverb

### Who's got the power?

The word 'error' does not denote something that is 'wrong' exactly, and should not make you feel defensive, as if you have made a mistake. Rather it is to do with making a **reality check**, of needing a **reinterpretation** of the **meaning** you have given to **events** in your daily life so far. According to CBT, 'thinking errors' can cause damage by helping sustain the powerless behaviour and thoughts you may be assuming are inevitable in your life. The purpose of CBT is to enable you to reveal to yourself your thinking errors, and to correct them, so that you can go on to have a better, more fulfilling, less weighed-down, and productive life. You have the power, if you can only see clearly enough to realise it.

## Beck's negative 'Cognitive Triad'

Beck invented a map of how our negative 'thinking errors' keep us from moving forward – the 'Cognitive Triad'. For instance, Prakesh is trying hard to be a good manager at work, but keeps losing his temper. When he barks orders the staff ignore him or withdraw, so his fury has the opposite effect of what he really wants to happen – which is an increase in production.

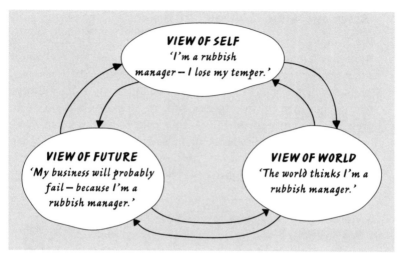

*Prakesh's negative Cognitive Triad*

# Top ten 'thinking errors'

The following ten categories give a rough guide to the common 'thinking errors' that CBT believes regularly occur in our negative perspectives. There is an inevitable amount of overlap between these types of 'thinking error', but teasing them out from your own Thought Record can help you track down what your own might well be.

1. 'Black and white thinking'.
2. 'Overgeneralisation'.
3. 'Mental filtering'.
4. 'Disqualifying the positive'.
5. 'Mind reading'/'fortune telling'.
6. 'Magnification' – 'catastrophising' (and 'minimising' – 'denying')
7. 'Emotional reasoning'/'magical thinking'.
8. 'Conditional thinking – making "should" statements'.
9. 'Personalising'.
10. 'Blaming and labelling'.

## 1. 'Black and white thinking': *To me, it's all or nothing ...'*

Black and white thinking is extremely polarised and leads to thoughts such as *'You're with us or you're against us'*, or *'You're either right or wrong'*. People with black and white, *'All or nothing'*, 'thinking errors' fall into the trap of thinking everything can be neatly packaged up into 'good' and 'bad'. There is little or no grey area in between. Although this kind of thinking can make for very effective politicians, business chiefs and leaders, it can be dangerous in that it leaves no room for the ambiguous areas in between the polar opposites of black and white.

Bernadette, 38, runs a corner-shop florist with an old friend from school, Daisy, 37. Bernadette is very exacting and likes to be in charge. She does the ordering, bookkeeping and runs the business paperwork; while Daisy does the arranging, window design and is better at dealing with the public. One day Bernadette is off sick (a rare occurrence), and Daisy is in charge. Daisy orders some extra red gerberas as they are very popular and on special offer at the market. Usually Daisy would check with Bernadette, but as she's sick she doesn't bother her. At the back of her mind, Daisy is a bit worried about Bernadette's reaction, but Daisy also knows a good deal when she sees one.

However, on her return to work the next day, Bernadette is livid about the extra order, and change of routine (even though the gerberas sold out). Instead of seeing Daisy as being helpful, she sees her as being interfering. Bernadette can't let herself see that Daisy got a good deal and used her initiative, rather; she is more worried about asserting her role as manager and keeping tight control.

Bernadette doesn't say 'Thank you' to Daisy for holding the fort, rather she nitpicks over and over about the order, making Daisy feel small for getting something 'wrong' (which she clearly didn't). This sends out a signal to Daisy – stay in your role and never take the initiative. Daisy sulks, feeling resentful. Her reaction also reinforces Bernadette's black and white way of doing business, which swipes aside any creativity from staff. In the long term this attitude will prove to be very damaging and expensive, especially when Daisy leaves to set up her own business.

The problem with *all or nothing* thinking is that it leaves no margin for subtlety or gradation. It can be very rigid, unforgiving and fixed. Life is much more complicated than this kind of thinking can cope with. Thus, people who think and behave in a black and white kind of way can find the complexities of life quite challenging.

For instance, if you wanted to work out which children in a classroom were 'good' and which were 'bad', and you made them line up in the playground, according to their labels, you would probably find it hard to work out where the two categories met. Each child would have some good, some bad in them, to differing degrees, meaning there would be a lot of ambiguity to deal with. Black and white thinkers typically find ambiguity extremely hard to handle.

While this kind of definite thinking can seem 'strong' and 'principled' it can also lead to radical and/or reactionary perspectives. Wars and family feuds emanate from a rigid black and white perspective that takes no prisoners (literally). When it's seen to be 'weak' to admit to the grey areas in between, the only way is to be on one side or the other. (Divorce or embattled business partnerships can also be like this.) The danger is you can fail to see some valuable, alternative mid-field perspectives and solutions when you are so busy making everything polarised into 'all or nothing'.

## Change checker

**Testing 'black and white thinking'**

- Watch out for black and white extremes in your thinking, using definitive language such as 'have to', 'should', 'must', 'ought'.

- Try stepping in the shoes of the opposing viewpoint, and see what your own perspective looks like – are there any similarities? What are the differences?

- Try saying 'it's complicated' to yourself, and tease out the 'in between' areas in your mind, or on paper.

- Next time you find yourself defending a 'right' perspective, count to ten, and allow yourself to wonder if there are any other viewpoints to consider.

## Insight

**Finding the midpoint**

You might feel you are clinging on to your black or white perspective for dear life because it is a matter of 'principle', or 'strength of character'. Remember there are more than two ways of looking at anything, plus there can be severe psychological damage done by making everything 'all or nothing'. Instead of thinking in extremes, try to think about things lying somewhere on a continuum – try testing out your ideas, by moving them more towards the middle. It may feel strange at first, but it's worth playing with to create change.

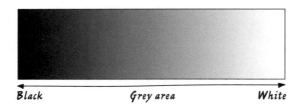

Black         *Grey area*         *White*

## 2. 'Overgeneralisation': *'Just my luck, something always goes wrong ...'*

If you 'overgeneralise' you take one fact and make it into a rule that totally runs your life. You lose at a game of squash and say *'I'm hopeless at all sports, I'm giving up...'*; or your friend forgets to ring you when they said they would, and you conclude *'... I know s/he hates me'*. Overgeneralisation means, literally, that the smallest thing leads to a conclusion where everything is included. It is the mountain-out-of-a-molehill mentality.

If you overgeneralise, you like to feel you can predict accurately what will happen to you, based on what has already happened. You may do this for a (false) sense of security – so then there will be no nasty surprises ahead. For instance, when you don't get included in the group going for drinks in the pub after work, you tell yourself (defensively), *'There, I knew it: I'm the least popular person at work – I'll never make friends or succeed now'*. If you believe this statement, you will inevitably act, think and behave in ways which will bring about that cataclysmic conclusion. You'll be offhand with people, push people away, sulk – all of which will probably lead to you being left out of the drinks next time around.

Overgeneralisation creates the *'self-fulfilling prophecy'* typical of a need to somehow control painful outcomes. By explaining to yourself that you are not liked at work, you can give up trying, so that you no longer get invited. You then think *'Aha, I knew it'* and it becomes a negative, vicious circle. Eeyore's black thoughts creating more black outcomes all over again.

Each month when Doreen, 25, got a flyer in her inbox inviting her to drinks in a central city pub with old university friends, she deleted it. She told herself *'They don't really want me to go'* or *'They're only taking pity on me, I was never that popular'*. So each month the date of the reunion would pass, and Doreen would blank it, deliberately. It didn't include her. She did feel a niggle deep down, but she squashed those feelings as being 'silly'.

Then one Saturday she bumped into one of her old uni friends, Cleo. They chatted briefly and as Doreen turned to leave Cleo said, *'By the way, why don't you ever come to the drinks? Aren't we good enough for you now?'* 'What?' exclaimed Doreen, totally surprised. *'Surely it's the other way round – I don't think you really want me there'.* 'What on earth makes you say that?' It was Cleo's turn to exclaim now. *'Why on earth do you think you're invited if we don't want to see you? There are plenty of people we haven't invited'.*

Doreen's jaw dropped. She'd never thought of it that way, as she was so busy thinking that she knew exactly what people thought about her. She finally had to admit she was wrong. Next month, she decided to go, but she felt really nervous. Doreen then realised, reluctantly, it was her own shyness about going out, not her friends' reluctance to invite her, that was the real root of the problem.

## Change checker

**Do you overgeneralise?**

- Do you find yourself overgeneralising from minimal evidence? If so, try to keep an open mind, and look at what you think about a situation first.

- Do you ever think you can read people's minds? If so, countenance the fact that you may get it completely wrong. There may be things happening behind the scenes that you simply know nothing about. So try to keep an open mind.

**"**A man can only do what he can do. But if he does that each day he can sleep at night and do it again the next day.**"**

**Albert Schweitzer**

3. **'Mental filtering':** *'I told you so … I knew it would happen …'*

'Filtering' is when we literally weed out things that fail to fit with our negative perspective. It's something we all do from time to time, and is a particularly destructive 'thinking error'. It's like your mind is a giant colander, only letting through some of the things that are poured in. If you filter your thoughts in this way, you will reinforce your negative cognitions, as you pick out only the pessimistic things that fit your world view, and throw any other perspective away.

Thomas, a retired accountant in his late sixties, thinks nobody likes him. He has become fairly isolated since his wife died, as he has holed himself up in his house, refusing invitations to dinner or for weekends away. Thomas keeps the answerphone on 24/7. Gradually people have got the message that he 'wants to be alone', growing his veg on the allotment. Meanwhile, deep down, Thomas feels lonely, and afraid of growing old. His only son, Greg, organises a birthday party and eventually people gather. Only a few come, not sure of his welcome. After the gathering, which has been a great success, Thomas turns to his son (who has worked hard to organise the event) and says, *'See, I told you no one would come'.*

The damage done to the father–son relationship is great here, as Greg feels hugely undervalued. Thomas also reduces his own capacity for happiness, as he fails to appreciate the people who actually made the effort to come to his birthday – and only pays attention to the absentees. He is filtering out the positive, thereby reinforcing his negative state as isolated and unlovable.

Thomas' core beliefs of *'I am unlovable'* and *'I am worthless'* are strongly reinforced by his only noticing who did not make the effort to come, rather than those who did. If he could allow himself to really see how far people had travelled, acknowledge that they had dressed up, hired babysitters, bought presents, it might help him to realise that he was lovable and worth something after all. The question is whether his 'filtering thinking error' – which he is clinging on to grimly himself – will let him contemplate these kinds of positive thoughts.

---

## Change checker

**Do you filter your thoughts?**

- Do you ever find yourself 'filtering' out the good things in order to focus on the negative? If you do, try to balance them by noticing more positives to redress the imbalance.

- Ever fasten on to one or two things as a way of taking your eye off the bigger picture? If so, try to expand your perspective – look wider than you are comfortable with and learn to pat yourself on the back when you do.

- Can you work out when you tend to react in this way? You can begin to spot patterns, such as tending to filter out when people think well about you, or cheer on your successes.

---

## 4. 'Disqualifying the positive': 'Yes, but it was nothing really ...'

This thinking is quite subtle, but has a devastating effect. It has a 'drip, drip' effect of wearing down your own self-confidence and self-esteem. It can be a very frustrating thing for other people around you, if you will never, ever take any credit for your own efforts. This 'thinking error' shifts the emphasis on to someone else, as a defence against getting attention or being positive. It can become quite an annoying pattern for other people to deal with – especially if you also apply it to them and their efforts. It can end up seeming like you are mega-critical of everything, and suck the joy and happiness out of life.

> **Insight**
>
> **Have you ever 'disqualified the positive'?**
>
> Think of a time, at work, where you have achieved something: met a target, written a report, handled a difficult meeting. When your boss or colleague tried to congratulate you, you brushed them off, saying, *'It was nothing'*. If you have done this on behalf of your team, your colleagues could well feel aggrieved. If you disqualify the positive, you are actually minimising your achievements, and devaluing them. It can mean you fail to value the achievements of others, because you minimise these too. And if you do it with children, it can really damage their self-confidence, self-esteem and self-worth.
>
> Jarvis, 35, likes to think of himself as a good person. His mother wanted her flat painted, and so Jarvis persuaded his partner, Denise, to paint it with him one bank holiday weekend. It was a long, hard slog of a weekend, which had had its fun and frustrating moments. Then Jarvis's mother offered to take them out for a meal as a 'thank you', which Denise thought was great. *'No, Ma, it was nothing'*, said Jarvis, *'You keep your money,'* which was a fine sentiment from Jarvis towards his mother, but which left Denise seething. After all, she'd given up her weekend and she felt very taken for granted by Jarvis. She could actually have done with a nice meal out after all that work.

## 5. 'Mind reading/fortune telling': *I know they don't like me ...'*

'Mind reading' – also commonly known as 'jumping to conclusions' – is something many of us do from time to time, and it can be quite destructive if we continually get it wrong. It's essentially a defensive behaviour, born of trying to protect ourselves against attack. The problem is that it can be incredibly inaccurate, even 'paranoid'. If we fail to ask people what they really think (assuming we will believe them), we can throw at them all sorts of imaginative fantasies about what the real meaning of their behaviour, words and actions, is. We can spend a lot of time 'double guessing' what's in their minds, unable to check the reality. This 'thinking error' is the arch enemy of reason, in that it makes huge assumptions about other people, the world, everything and anything, in order to fit in with its negative viewpoint.

## Insight

**Women 'mind readers' alert**

Women are particularly prone to mind reading, although not exclusively, as some men obviously do it, too. Within a circle of women friends, at work or at home, there can be all sorts of assumptions about what a look or gesture means. Women are constantly trying to fathom out what people think about them, or feel about them, from 'clues'. The thing is they can get it horribly wrong, without being able to check it out: so regular reality checks are essential. Ask your friends and colleagues what they really think – and listen carefully to what they answer.

## Change checker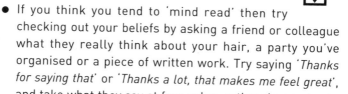

- If you think you tend to 'mind read' then try checking out your beliefs by asking a friend or colleague what they really think about your hair, a party you've organised or a piece of written work. Try saying *'Thanks for saying that'* or *'Thanks a lot, that makes me feel great'*, and take what they say at face value, rather than trying to delve into what the 'double meaning' might actually be.

> • Try and quell any 'fortune-telling' tendencies you might
> have by limiting your views to the present time. If you are
> able to check out what someone thinks about your new
> suit, or your job application, try not to let your mind run
> on to what it might mean in the future. You are bound to
> be inaccurate as you will be projecting your ideas, rather
> than checking out the facts.

## 6. 'Magnification' – 'catastrophising' (and 'minimising' – 'denying'): *'It's the end of the world ...'*

Magnification, more commonly known as 'catastrophising', is when you make not only a mountain out of a proverbial mole-hill, but a volcano that erupts and completely destroys the world – nay, the entire universe. Like this last description, catastrophising knows no bounds: everything is terrible, really awful, disastrous, and there are no real variations in degree of difficulty. The real trouble with catastrophising, or making things as bad as they can possibly be, is that it means there is no way of really assessing how terrible something actually is.

If you catastrophise, then the accompanying, exaggerated sense of gloom and doom means that you are scared to the maximum all the time. You are constantly tense and wary, with the 'flight or fight' mechanism at the ready, as everything that comes your way is labelled a 'disaster: the end of the world'. The problem with this thinking error is there is no judgement involved in weighing up just how difficult or dangerous any situation is.

If you are launched into a complete disaster zone every time anything happens, you spend your life wearing yourself out, and wearing others' compassion out. It's the 'cry wolf' syndrome – and everyone ends up with 'compassion fatigue'. Also, if everything is always the worst that it can be – what do you do when a real disaster actually comes along?

Conversely, 'minimisers' deny that things are bad, and try to make everything the same. This means that in an emergency they hardly respond, as they are continuing to flatten our their emotional reactions. This defensive behaviour can be quite dangerous in itself, in that it does not respond appropriately when things go wrong. A thinking error that denies can lead to procrastination as well as an inability to handle what life throws at you.

Vivienne woke late, got stuck in traffic and was already running half an hour late for work. Panicking, she thought: *'Oh no! I'm late for the meeting ... and my boss will sack me and I'll lose my job. Then my flat will be repossessed as I won't be able to pay the mortgage – and I'll never get another job. Then I'll be thrown out and on the street, with nowhere to go, and my boyfriend will leave me ... I'll never have children or happiness, my parents with disown me, and my life will be over. It's all hopeless, so I might as well crash my car into a wall right now! How could I have done this to myself? If only I'd left earlier, if only I'd not taken my short cut, if only I'd got up an hour earlier, and not watched that show last night and not had that extra glass of wine – I've ruined everything ...'*

You can see the snowballing effect of 'catastrophising', as everything gets thrown into maximum panic, which mounts and mounts, like a snowball of fear rolling forward, gathering everything in its path.

On the other hand, a minimiser's response to getting stuck in a traffic jam might be: *'never mind ... I'll get there at some point ... who cares?'* And thus would fail to make the necessary calls, or to handle the situation powerfully and diplomatically, hence bringing about reprisals, such as actually losing a job or friends.

---

### Change checker

**Do you catastrophise? Or minimise?**

- Think about an occasion when something has gone wrong – have you been able to think in the situation or has your panic snowballed? Could you stand back – right now – and think how you might react to a similar situation to the future?

- If you minimise things when they go wrong, could you react more appropriately? What would you have to face to let yourself see the difficulties for real?

---

7. **'Emotional reasoning'/'magical thinking'**: *I'm responsible for everything that happens' or 'everything happens for a reason ...'*

This is a very common 'thinking error', and most of us will do it at some time or another. If you have children – or you work with them – you will see them doing this all the time. It is quite a narcissistic viewpoint, where you believe that you have 'caused' something to happen by merely thinking it.

**Examples of 'emotional reasoning':**

- **Ben feels guilty** → So he assumes he must have done something wrong.
- **Prathi feels angry** → So she thinks it will thunder today.
- **Delia feels panicky** → So she absolutely knows something terrible is about to happen.
- **Jim feels fat** → So he's sure he looks like a house.

This kind of 'thinking error' is based on believing there is a causative link. Yet it might well be illogical or magical thinking, and does not make sense at all under closer examination. It's easy to think this way, especially if you have convinced yourself that in life there is always a simple cause-and-effect relationship between your thoughts and their apparent outcomes.

You may have grown up with people who think like this, or have developed a habit of always linking the two things – your thought (*'I feel lonely'*) and what you believe to be reality (*'I am totally alone'*). You may be in a roomful of people, feeling lonely – when in fact you could reach out and make contact, if you weren't telling yourself you were *'totally alone'*.

---

Jill gets a huge credit card bill in the post. She looks out of the window and it starts raining heavily. *'See, it's just not my day'*, thinks Jill, *'things come in threes, so there's bound to be something else that goes wrong'*.
Just as she is going out of the door, she drops a mug of coffee and it splashes her dress. *'There, I knew it wasn't going to be*

*my day'*. Jill has linked all three events together – the credit card bill, the rain and the spilled coffee. But are they linked? Could it be that her preoccupation with the bill and how much she has spent recently have simply made her fearful and prone to watch out for 'bad' things? The more she looks for connections between things the more she will see them. It's another self-fulfilling prophecy – and we do it everyday.

---

### Change checker

**Look out for your emotional reasoning**

- Do you ever make connections between things, no matter how irrational (touching wood, etc.)? What would it feel like not to make these connections?

- Have you noticed how often things don't work out according to your predictions? Try and notice them in future … and keep your mind more open to things happening for different, even random, reasons.

- Ask yourself – would someone else react to the same situation in the same way?

---

### Insight

**Be rational about emotions**

- Can you think of a time when you felt a certain way and then found out it was not really the case (such as feeling guilty, and then finding out you weren't actually to blame)?

- What would you have to do to stop emotional reasoning being the way you look at the world?

- If you feel sure your interpretation is the right one – can you step back, mentally, and imagine three other possible explanations? If so, this can help loosen up this kind of thinking error.

## 8. 'Conditional thinking – making "should" statements':
*'I must be nice to people, or they'll …'*

This thinking error is extremely fixed and rigid: full of 'shoulds', 'oughts', 'musts' and 'never'. Typical examples are:

- *'I **should** be on time all the time, then I'll be loved …'*
- *'I'll **never** be good enough for her, until I'm rich …'*
- *'I **ought** to be a better son and father. …'*

These 'should-based' NATs reveal typical **core beliefs** of 'I am unlovable' or 'I am worthless'. Conditional thinking is punitive, destructive and can be very resistant (but not impossible) to being shifted into a more positive viewpoint. Often conditional statements, lead to rigid, negative thought processes.

Sometimes people with OCD feel they have to do certain things, or perform certain rituals, to stop something dreadful happening. This can lead to a very 'should-based' thinking error. One woman I saw for counselling had to check her handbag for her keys three times before she could leave home, and then, on leaving, had to go back and check the front door was really locked three more times.

On the one hand it might seem weird to be this obsessive, but to my client it seemed perfectly natural. She was not sure, even when she checked the keys or the door, whether it was really locked or not. In the moment of checking, her fear levels were so high and she was so preoccupied that afterwards she couldn't really remember doing it. So she had to do it again.

Although this is an extreme example, and obviously not everyone is OCD, there is an element in how we can all think here. We can be driven by feelings of fear, uncertainty, anxiety or confusion to do all sorts of things, and put ourselves under immense strain as a consequence.

**Insight**

Mind the 'should' trap

Try noticing how often you paint yourself into a corner with your 'shoulds', 'musts' and 'oughts'. Try to drop these kinds of conditional statements, or backtrack when you are thinking that way. 'Shoulds' can become an emotional straitjacket, making other solutions to problems seem unappealing or out of reach. You need to give yourself a chance to think outside the rigidity of the 'should' statement to find other answers, or allow other viewpoints on a situation to emerge. The root of a lot of should statements is guilt or even anger, and acting on these feelings seldom gets us very far.

## 9. 'Personalising': *I'll never be good enough ...'*

It's very easy to take things personally in a negative way and this kind of thinking error can lead us to believing that everything that happens is about us, somehow, and in some destructive kind of way. *'She always picks on me, it's all my fault ...'* or *'I'm never chosen for a dance, it must be my looks ...'* or *'I feel excruciatingly embarassed every time he comes in the room...'.* These kinds of thoughts point to everything being about you, everything being personal and pointed. In this situation the person needs to evaluate:

- Who else is picked on ... is it *really* just you?
- *Are* you the only one not asked to dance?
- Are you *really* stared at when someone comes in the room?

**Reality check**

Do you 'personalise'?

Think of a time when you have felt something is happening in your life, which is personal to you. It may be a situation at work, with a friend, with a partner or with someone in your family. Do you feel singled out for special treatment? Or do you think it's possible the person who makes you feel that way might be treating other people similarly? Try and see things from a cooler, more rational perspective – and try not to personalise things if you can.

## 10. 'Blaming and labelling'

Blame is the ultimate way of avoiding responsibility for something. It is negative, destructive and means you can stay extremely stuck in whatever patterns are running and ruining your life. Putting the blame on to others, making everything 'someone's else's fault' means you stay stuck yourself. You don't grow if you don't shoulder responsibility. Blaming thinking errors are defensive in the extreme, and can push people away. Thoughts such as *'It's not my fault'* or *'How could they do this to me?'*, leave you feeling extremely powerless.

The flip side to blaming is to be over-responsible for everything. Again, this can be the case for people who have OCD, who tend to feel hugely guilty and responsible for absolutely everything. This can lead to a need for utter perfection (unattainable, of course), and then self-punishment, when that unattainable perfection is not attained.

Also, 'labelling' means you see things (rather like the 'black and white' thinking error) in fairly simplistic terms. People are 'bad' or 'good' or 'lazy' or 'evil'. Once labelled it is difficult to shift the idea – (*'If I'm not that kind of person, then I'm utterly unlovable'*; or *'If I'm not the best employee, I'm totally useless'*. If you give yourself the label of useless or unlovable, it may stick and you may not be able to allow yourself to see round it at all.

Miriam, 45, tends to blame her husband for everything. Somehow, during their 15-year marriage, they have settled into a pattern where, whatever goes wrong, Miriam attacks Jeremy, 50, who then tries to make it all better. Only recently did Jeremy begin to fight back, when Miriam's demands became more unreasonable than ever. He had booked a holiday to Greece, and when they got there the room was in a villa facing a building site. Miriam moaned, attacked and criticised, calling Jeremy everything she could think of. *'How could he have been so stupid as to book a villa facing a wall?'*

Jeremy had tried hard to give Miriam what she wanted (after a lot of carping), and he obviously hadn't booked a room facing a wall deliberately. He was as upset about it as she was. It was just that her feelings took precedence, as always. And she used her disappointment to belittle and humiliate him. Jeremy, usually mild-mannered, found himself shouting back that he'd had enough of Miriam's constant abuse and was leaving. He strode out of the villa and walked for miles. On his return, very late that night, Miriam was quiet for once. *'I thought you'd gone and left me here,'* she said meekly, in tears.

Although Miriam found it hard to say a proper 'Sorry' she was finally able to acknowledge, albeit grudgingly, that she had been too harsh. *'I'm sick of you blaming me for everything'*, said Jeremy finally. *'I've had enough. You can book the next holiday'*. Miriam had to agree reluctantly that Jeremy had a point. She never took responsibility, would just rather attack him for getting things wrong. She felt too intimidated by dealing with travel agents or the Internet to book a holiday herself. Finally, she agreed to try to stop blaming him for everything. Jeremy agreed to stay for the rest of the holiday. Together, they went to see the villa owner and got themselves moved to another site.

## Your CBT change toolkit

Tool no. 1: Make and stick with your decision to change.

Tool no. 2: Understand how you interpret the world and how you 'tick'.

Tool no. 3: Notice and note down negative thoughts.

**Tool no. 4: Track down and eliminate your thinking errors**

## Homework

Keep your Thought Record over a week or two weeks. Then sit down and look at the kinds of NATs that keep occurring. Can you see any patterns? Are you aware of any 'thinking errors' that crop up over and over again? If so, you can begin to build a picture of the kinds of things that you are preoccupied with, or the way you think about things. Make a second list of how many times you find yourself falling into these kinds of 'thinking errors' over a day. Only when you start to see what you are doing can you begin to do something to correct it.

**Chapter**

# 5

'The reason you haven't heard of it, Mr Scott, is because you haven't discovered it yet.'

Spock, *Star Trek*

# Testing yourself to get better

Ever seen an episode of the original *Star Trek*? If so, you'll know that the 'pointy-eared' star of the show is Spock, the half-human, half-Vulcan 'science officer' who serves under Captain Kirk. Spock is renowned for remaining cool, detached and calm in all crises – despite his vulnerable human side. He is also known for analysing problems at breakneck speed, announcing *'It's logical, Captain'* .

CBT asks you to take on a Spock-like role in order to analyse your own problems. You will be asked to examine yourself anew as you try to pinpoint your own difficulties from a more detached perspective.

An important element of CBT involves creating tests to help you move forward. You may feel this is (literally) alien to how you might usually operate, or that you don't have time to conduct experiments on yourself in your busy life. However, it's probably worth opening your mind to the possibility of trying by following the suggestions in this book, if you really want things to change. The best way to do this for yourself is to break things down into manageable, bite-sized chunks – which is exactly how CBT works.

**❝**Knowing yourself is the beginning of all wisdom.**❞**     Aristotle

---

### Reality check

**Breaking down your responses**

To recap briefly about the essential elements of CBT we've met in the previous four chapters:

▶

1. We have identified:
   - negative automatic thoughts;
   - dysfunctional assumptions.
2. Which reveal our:
   - core beliefs.

And that

3. the accumulation of these can lead to us developing longer-term psychological patterns, or:
   - thinking errors.

If you are still unclear about these ideas, have a quick look back at the previous four chapters, and review any homework you have done so far. It will help you to keep the concepts in mind as we move forward in this chapter.

## Hot thoughts and triggers

Approaching your difficulties with Spock-like coolness, it's important to begin to locate what **hot thoughts** or **triggers** can set off your emotions, moods or behaviour. Triggers will ignite your negative thoughts and behaviours almost before you have had a chance to notice them or think consciously about the situation.

You might think it's difficult to catch things before you are aware of them, but in time you should accumulate enough knowledge about yourself to know what to avoid, and what to scorn. Once you can begin to recognise your reactions to your triggers you will be much more in the driving seat in your life. This is because you will be attempting to make things that are usually unconscious and hidden, actually conscious and open.

Your unbidden responses hark back to the 'fight or flight' reactions we all experience through our autonomous nervous systems and which are there to keep us safe. Triggers are things that happen repeatedly, and are your emotional 'Achilles heel', so it's important to start noticing what sets you off with as much accuracy as you can.

The forensic CBT part is to keep writing things down in your Thought Record, so you can check back to how you felt in various situations in your daily life. You can begin to piece together a picture of your triggers, which then begins to help you formulate your blueprint for change.

For instance, Mary told me that she has a difficult relationship with her father. They always argue, as they have always done, even though she is now in her forties and he's in his seventies. She has noticed, after keeping her Thought Record for six months, that when she visits him her stomach starts tightening up and she gets generally tense and tetchy. *'I get this sort of irritable feeling'*, she explains, *'and it's as if I'm spoiling for a fight. I get headachey and narky, and I realise that I am in "that" mood because I know my old dad is going to wind me up.'* Mary is trying hard not to get wound up. She says their relationship has been bad for years.

Now Mary's finally decided that she wants it to be better, and that it's clear he won't or can't change. Mary realises now that the only thing that can change is her reaction to her father. *'I estimate how I feel before I visit, and usually it's 90 per cent tense,'* she explains, *'but afterwards the anxiety has dropped to 50 per cent, so I can see that seeing him is better than pretending he's not there.'* She also notices she is letting go of any things she would usually react to because she is simply more aware of them now. *'He always goes on that I should have had children or got married,'* says Mary, *'and I now ignore it. I don't engage and he gives up, so we don't argue any more about my single life'.*

It can be difficult to pinpoint your hot thoughts and triggers yourself, but it will be essential for you to become aware of them so you can work out what needs to change. You might find that your hot thoughts cluster around certain things – so if you are socially anxious your 'hot thoughts' might be triggered by going to a party, walking into a room alone, standing up in front of an audience, presenting a report at work, or simply trying to say 'hello' to a stranger.

It's important for you to collect up your 'triggers' once you've started spotting them. They may lead you to understand your difficulties better because they will probably reveal a common theme in your psychological make-up.

**Here are some examples of triggers from different people, taken from real life:**

- You are sitting at a traffic light in your car, and a street window cleaner approaches and starts sponging your windscreen, unmasked – you feel a sudden rush of anger, and want to drive off or even hurt them.

- You are sitting on a train platform, and as the train comes in, you have a sudden compulsion to jump up and throw yourself under it – you have to grip yourself hard to hold back from doing so.

- Someone pushes in front of you in a queue. You've been waiting for ten minutes, and are late, and you suddenly feel like grabbing them or shouting.

- You wake up in a bad mood, somewhat hungover, and the minute someone speaks to you, you feel like it's too much effort to concentrate, so you feel like withdrawing (or shouting).

- Your boss puts you under pressure. You have to complete another piece of work, out of work hours, as a deadline has to be met. You would like to say 'No' but you feel you can't, so you put yourself under pressure to meet the deadline, hoping you will get extra praise or pay, without negotiating either.

- Your mother-in-law is visiting, so you scrub the house from top to bottom, get in all her favourite food, cook her ideal meal, in the hope that you will please her – or at least allay any criticism – you really need things to be absolutely perfect.

- The children rush in from the garden, put their muddy feet all over your newly cleaned floor and hug you with muddy hands, and you feel utterly contaminated – all that dirt and mess in your nice clean kitchen.

- You go to a party with your partner and they start talking avidly to a member of the opposite sex (who is very attractive) while you are huddled in a corner. After a while you are boiling with jealousy and all you can think about is yanking your partner away and taking them home ... you are on the verge of making a big scene.

This list could go on, but it is an attempt to show you the kinds of everyday moments that might occur (you will have your own and many more besides) which can set off a reaction in you emotionally.

**Hot thoughts**, typically:

● trigger a negative emotional response

● trigger a negative behaviour

● trigger a change in your mood.

**Here are two more examples of common triggers set out in a CBT way for Spock-like analysis:**

| Nathan's triggers | Common theme | Problem |
|---|---|---|
| 1. The doorbell ringing unexpectedly<br>2. Being asked to the pub after work<br>3. His wife inviting people for dinner | Fear of being in social situation | Social anxiety |
| **Sami's triggers** | **Common theme** | **Problem** |
| 1. Finding cat sick in the hall<br>2. Making a mistake making bread for supper<br>3. Not getting the washing finished | Unforgiving of mistakes | Perfectionism, OCD |
| **Your triggers** | **Common theme** | **Problem** |
| 1.<br><br>2.<br><br>3. | | |

# Understanding your own CBT 'formulation'

What we are going to do now is formulate a blueprint about you: work out best how to move things forward for you. So sharpen your pencils, boot up your computer, open your Apps, and off we go.

## Break it down into bite-sized bits

When you spot a trigger, as in any of the scenarios above, then you will have direct access to your NATs as they float to the surface of your mind immediately, like froth on the top of the glass.

Start 'thinking about your thinking': it's very useful to break down your response into smaller bits, so that you can begin to 'see' what's happening.

Say you are terrified of getting into a car and driving (or even being a passenger) because you had a nasty accident a few years ago. Someone asks if you need a lift in their car. There's your trigger. To break down your response, the CBT approach would be to get you to look at your experience from four different angles:

1. **Your cognitions (what you are thinking)** The words that go through your mind as you imagine getting in the car, or sitting in the passenger seat, or even getting behind the wheel. These might be *'I'd rather die rather than get into a car again ...'*, or *'I keep seeing the accident when I imagine sitting in the driver's seat ...'*.

2. **Your emotions (how you are feeling)** How you feel, such as 'frightened', 'anxious', 'worried' or 'scared'. (Emotions are usually just a word – if you say 'I think I'm scared' – that's describing a thought, not a feeling).

3. **Your behaviour (what you are doing)** Have you stopped going near the car and instead walk everywhere, or take public transport? Do you refuse lifts? Are you making excuses when your partner asks you to take the wheel? Behaviour covers everything that is outwardly visible – what you do or do not do.

4. **Your bodily responses (how you are feeling physically)** If you are feeling scared, thinking about driving, or being near a car, you may experience a racing heart, sweaty hands, shaking limbs, nausea, aching muscles – all *autonomic* responses to fear. You may experience this even before you consciously think or are able to catch your 'black bat' thoughts or feelings as they flit through your mind.

## Understanding your triggers

Take a situation that you know will be difficult for you, such as map reading in a car, or going out with friends if you feel shy, or something that might happen soon that you are dreading, and try filling in the following headings:

1. Your **cognitions** (what you are thinking)

2. Your **emotions** (what you are feeling)

3. Your **behaviour** (what you are doing)

4. Your **bodily responses** (how you are doing physically.

**❝**What lies behind us, and what lies before us are tiny matters, compared to what lies within us.**❞**                    Ralph Waldo Emerson

---

### Test yourself

**How to formulate your problems (Spock-style)**

For CBT to work you will need to adopt a Spock-like perspective to the following:

● Describe the problem you have – using your own words, especially describing how the negative emotions, thoughts and behaviours affect your life.

● Test the validity of a negative thought or belief that you have about yourself and/or the world.

● Discover how your thinking, feelings and behaviour continue to maintain your difficulties.

---

- Keep gathering evidence as to how all of these things keep your problems in place.

- Keep experimenting with changing your thinking, emotions and behaviour, which in turn will affect your feelings, behaviour and thoughts.

- Regularly review your progress and keep adjusting.

The reason for being so scientific about everything is because it is easy to be swamped by the number of negative assumptions that seem to distort our thinking, feelings and behaviour. By setting up real-time 'tests' we can work out what is real and what is not.

Many of our negative ideas are rooted in fear and anxiety, and if we test them experimentally we often find that what we have believed to be true simply is not. If you are always thinking the worst will happen, and you live life too carefully, it can be a real liberation to find out life is not as dangerous as you think it is. Taking risks or facing challanges can set you free.

## Here comes the science bit

### How CBT 'formulation' works

- You take your existing problem or difficulty (e.g. fear of going out at night).

- You 'formulate' a prediction about what would happen if you did something different about it in your life (change your behaviour, change your thinking, change your feelings) (*I will go out instead of staying in*').

- You conduct an experiment – you do something to check the reality of the situation, the thought, the feeling, the behaviour in the real world – a 'reality check' (*I will go out, with a friend, after dark*').

● You check out what happened afterwards– did your 'experiment' work? Did it change how you felt? Did it change your behaviour or the behaviour of others? Do you need to adjust anything? *('I was scared 90 per cent beforehand. Afterwards I felt it was more like 60 per cent dangerous.')*

At all times you need to be scoring yourself on a scale of, say, 0–10 or 0–100 per cent so you can see if something has changed.

## The 'Vicious Flower' exercise

There is another CBT exercise which can help to try and tease out the 'meanings' that underpin any particular emotional problem. The Vicious Flower exercise helps you pin down the thoughts, emotions, behaviours, physical sensations and attention focus that are set off by a particular trigger.

Charleen hates the phone ringing at home. She works in a frantic call-centre, and is on the phone, literally, all day. Once she gets home she wants peace and quiet, and the last thing she feels like doing is answering the phone. Charleen has also recently divorced, and her husband has been phoning to hassle her about money, so she has another reason to feel phobic about the phone. Her reactions are getting more intense, so Charleen decides to plot out her Vicious Flower so that she can see what's happening to her when the phone rings.

Charleen fills in the flower box with the trigger incident (the phone rings) and then each petal of the flower shows what's going on as things unfold.

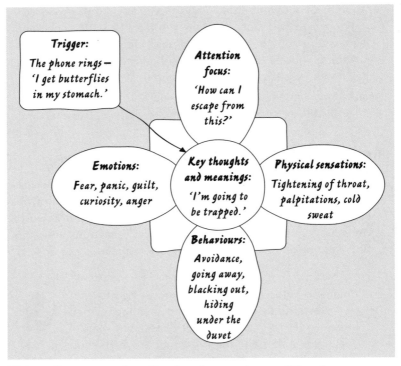

*Vicious flower exercise: Charleen's experience of the phone ringing at home*

### Test yourself

**Now you try**

If there is something that triggers a distress response in you, such as a child crying, noisy neighbours, demands from a partner, bills plopping on to the mat, seeing a daddy-long-legs in the bath, or bumping into an ex-partner, try filling in your own Vicious Flower. Start with your 'trigger'.

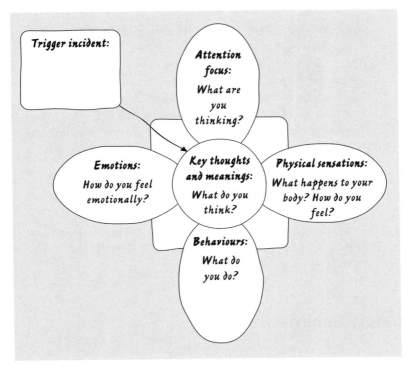

*Your vicious flower exercise*

## Emotional shifts

How tuned in are you with your emotions? How much are you aware of how you feel at any one moment? Are you conscious of your moods, and shifts of feelings as you go through the day? Can you put your finger on what triggers certain ups and downs that occur at work, on the street, at home? Sometimes our moods change, minute to minute, just going in the front door, or smelling a perfume, or when thunder claps and lightning strikes, or on seeing the expression on someone's face.

You can easily begin to descend into a downward spiral of gloom and doom, all triggered by that one 'hot thought' moment, say when no one noticed you come into the room. It may well be that you were deliberately not invited; or it could simply be an oversight (such as they didn't see you), so that is something you need to test scientifically.

You can also sense your reluctance to do something, as a sign of your fear. For instance, Barnaby feels terrified of going to the doctor's surgery. Whenever he has to go for an appointment he feels faint, so he tends to avoid his appointments. However, he has been ill recently, and he knows he has to go, but when he wakes up he begins to tell himself all the reasons why he doesn't actually need to go. This is the first moment he can sense his 'phobia' clicking into action: he feels sick, and actually on occasion has been sick, at the very thought of going to the doctor. He's also 'forgotten' his appointments sometimes, as his mind has blanked out his diary. So Barnaby knows if he's going to get himself to the doctor he will have to climb through some pretty difficult feelings of reluctance, fear, anxiety and nausea.

## Safety Behaviours

One of the central ideas in CBT is that we manage to *maintain* our problems ourselves, by doing, thinking, feeling, in certain ways. These are called **Safety Behaviours**. This sounds like CBT is blaming you – it's not. Rather it is saying that we all adopt certain ways of being which we think will make us feel comfortable. Ironically, although we adopt them because we believe they will ensure we feel OK, they can actually make our problems worse in the medium and even longer term because they keep us stuck.

*How Safety Behaviours work*

1. You are frightened about something/dislike the feelings.
2. You avoid confronting the situation, or exposing yourself to the feelings.
3. The situation remains unchallenged, so the feelings remain the same – unchallenged, buried, dormant, lurking – thus nothing changes.

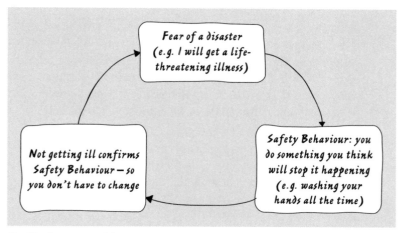

*Cyclical nature of 'Safety Behaviour': keeps everything the same*

**"**You must do the thing you think you cannot do.**"**

**Eleanor Roosevelt**

Richard is a very successful businessman. He has a fast car, a fabulous penthouse, a luxury boat, and spends a great deal of time on the road, travelling between high-level business meetings in Europe.

The problem is that Richard is severely claustrophobic. He has a chronic problem, emanating from childhood, when his parents used to lock him in a cupboard to punish him when he was 'naughty'. As an adult, Richard finds he is simply unable to go into any enclosed or subterranean space, such as underground trains and car parks, lifts or tunnels. As a consequence, whenever he is driving in France, Switzerland or Italy, he has to drive around the Alps and other mountain range, so as to avoid the tunnels.

However, Richard's Safety Behaviour (avoiding tunnels) means he spends much longer on the road, exposed to traffic wear and tear (and accidents); he's away from his family longer (his wife is fed up with his absences), and he can be late for meetings because of the traffic (his bosses are

▶

generally annoyed by his avoidance behaviour). In addition, his stress and weight levels are pretty high from so many hours sitting in the car. Of course, his fuel and hotel costs are astronomical, too, as his journeys take longer than they would if he went direct. In fact, the Safety Behaviour of avoiding the tunnels is putting his life in danger, on many significant fronts.

From a CBT perspective, Richard would need to experiment with going into enclosed spaces – albeit briefly at first – and monitoring his reactions (breathing, heart rate, panic) as a way of beginning to deal with his fear. Avoiding exposure to things he finds frightening is actually keeping his phobia of enclosed spaces in place.

## What about you?

Take a moment to think about things that you might be doing to avoid feelings? They could be something like these:

- opening and checking your bank statements (you hate facing money);
- not going dancing (you fear humiliation, having two left feet);
- not asking someone out for a date (don't want rejection);
- won't go swimming (hate showing your body off in public);
- can't have a pet (fear of birds goes back to childhood);
- hate touching food as it's 'dirty' or wet (phobia about illness).

Write down in your usual format any avoidance techniques you can think of that are true of you?

### Test yourself

**Your own Safety Behaviours**

Take a moment to think about your own Safety Behaviours. Are there any things that you do or think that:

- Maintain your fears?
- Keep you stuck?

- Reinforce any negative views you have of yourself?
- Reinforce any negative views you have of the world?
- Stop you trying something new? Or taking risks?

So, make a note of them.

Are there any consequences, which are not what you intended, when you do or think them? Any unwanted results or by-products? Again, make a note.

## Avoidance

Avoidance or escape is a classic Safety Behaviour. Johnny is terrified of playing guitar in public as he is sure he will forget the words and music. He loves guitar and he does it perfectly in the confines of his bedroom, but he believes he will go blank once on stage.

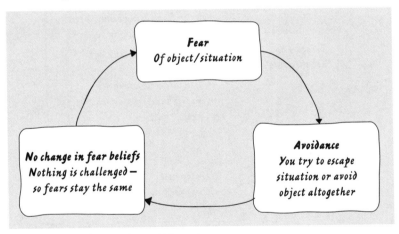

*Avoidance cycle: again, nothing changes*

It happened once when he was younger, and he felt intensely humiliated when he froze ('corpsed') on stage. The experience has stayed vividly with him ever since and, although it only happened once, that's been enough to put him off performing for life. Hence Johnny never plays in front of anyone else, even if friends are just 'jamming' together in his front room for fun.

The problem with avoidance is that it sets up a 'self-fulfilling prophecy' that is never tested, so Johnny will stay stuck, never being able to play in public.

Deep down he wishes desperately that he could be free of his terror, as he is missing opportunities to have fun with friends and forward his music career. But Johnny's desire to avoid repeating the bad experience of being publicly humiliated comes first.

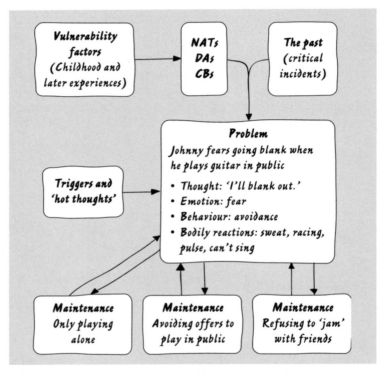

*Johnny's maintenance of his phobia through avoidance*

In order to break the grip avoidance will place on his personal growth Johnny would have to test out the NAT that he would always blank in public while playing guitar. To do this he'd have to put himself in a position of fear playing in front of someone (exposure). He could decide to start small, even by playing in front of the mirror, cat, a partner or his best friend. Just even holding the guitar in front of someone else might be the best place to start.

By testing his fear this way Johnny would inevitably begin to move himself forward: he would move out of the stuck position. He would begin to dismantle his own Safety Behaviour that is actually maintaining his problem. This would mean he could begin to change as his fear started to melt, like a great Antarctic iceberg.

# Exposure

A key part of learning to tackle problems experimentally in CBT is learning to **expose** yourself gradually to the very thing that you are worried about or are terrified of. In Richard's case, above, being 'exposed' to a lift or tunnel would mean going into an enclosed space for a short time, initially to see if he could survive intact.

At present his fear is so enormous that he can't imagine putting himself inside anything enclosed and dark. This fear makes him drive around the Alps and back to avoid it, and also risk his job, his marriage, and his health while he's at it. This only goes to show the power of the fear – and the enormity of the avoidance behaviour for 'safety reasons'. Thus, any experiment to try and wean Richard off his fear of expiring in a tunnel would need him, necessarily, to expose himself to the experience of going into an enclosed space.

While for Johnny 'exposing' himself by standing in front of the public with his guitar is enough to trigger off a panic attack. Yet it is precisely this that he will need to work towards doing, albeit step by step.

**Here's a step-by-step guide to how exposure works:**

1. When you first think about the thing that you are anxious about, say walking past a big dog, or speaking at a public meeting, your fear and anxiety level will probably be high (estimate 100 per cent anxiety);

2. Let's take being scared of a big dog: you might look at photos of dogs, or look at a dog – across the street, on a lead or in the window of a pet shop – and record how you feel (estimate 80 per cent anxiety).

3. After further thought you might actually be able to walk down the road, with a friend, who has a dog on a lead; or approach someone with a dog in the park (estimate 65 per cent anxiety).

4. Finally, you might even be able to form a fist with your hand and, after some emotional preparation, be able to let the dog sniff your fist (which is how they say 'Hello') or stroke a dog, or even take it for a very short walk (estimate 40 per cent anxiety).

At each stage of this kind of exposure you would measure your emotional reactions before, during and after the experience. The theory is, as you get used to the experience, and you learn that nothing untoward happens to you, you are able and willing to let yourself get even closer to the fearful experience – such as petting or walking a dog.

Notice the fear level went down from an all-out 100 per cent at the beginning to 40 per cent at the end, which means it dropped by over half. That is a significant and measurable result and something you can pat yourself on the back for achieving. The diagram below reflects how this works over time.

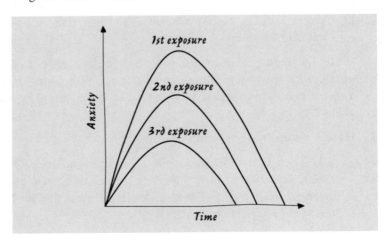

# Involving others

Sometimes it can feel too scary to do these kinds of experiments alone. You might feel too self-conscious, too silly or embarassed. The first tip is to start with something small and manageable. Say you are shy of going to a social event alone, try just going out for coffee with someone you know well, for half an hour, rather than going to a full-blown party or a long dinner with a stranger. You can build up to that over time. Starting small is usually a very good idea as it gets you used to being in a social situation.

## Suzi plays Spock

With 'exposure' techniques, you can be creative, ask friends or family to help you (if you don't want to go to a therapist). You'd be surprised at how much help people will willingly give you.

For instance, Suzi, 40, was very embarassed about her tendency to go bright red when she met people. It was so humiliating for her that she increasingly avoided people and any social situation where she might blush. This meant her life was shutting down horribly. Having thought about her 'triggers' (meeting strangers, going shopping), Suzi realised that she really needed to get out of the house, as she felt increasingly marooned and isolated. However, she felt daunted by this.

Suzi wondered about wearing a balaclava or scarf, but realised she would end up drawing more attention to herself. Suzi decided to test her embarassment. Finally, she decided to go out with a good friend, Mia, who could have an artificially induced florid complexion, so Suzi might be able to see objectively how other people reacted. She could do this safely without drawing attention to herself. The 'experiment' would also test how much attention florid cheeks actually drew from passers-by. It might help her to be more objective about how embarrassing her condition really was.

The test was this: would people stare and point at her friend, if her face was made very red artificially? Suzi imagined all sorts of terrible consequences of having a red face in public, and it made her pulse race and her palms sweat just thinking about it. Before they went out for a walk together Suzi rated her anxiety about her friend exposing her red cheeks to the public at an embarrassment level of 90 per cent. In other words, if it was Suzi doing it, she'd feel about 90% embarrassed.

So one sunny afternoon Mia visited Suzi, and Suzi rouged up Mia's cheeks, so she looked bright red (making them look just as Suzi *felt* hers looked when she was very embarrassed). Then together they walked to the local shops. Suzi wore dark glasses, as she felt shy just being out with Mia looking as she did. Suzi watched from behind her dark glasses to see how people reacted to Mia's bright red face. She was amazed when Mia was able to buy a newspaper and a bag of apples without any nasty comments or pointed stares. The newsagent said 'Hello' and treated Mia normally, as Suzi watched incredulously.

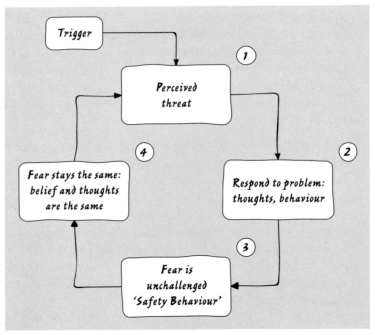

*Maintaining a problem with 'Safety Behaviour'*

Back home, Suzi and Mia discussed the situation and Suzi realised she now felt her own imagined embarrassment at going out with red cheeks was around 50–60 per cent, a significant drop from the 90 per cent she had felt before they went out. Suzi actually thought that next time she could even go out herself, alone, and risk going red, having seen the lack of pointing and staring at Mia's predicament. This was a major step forward and the beginning of Suzi getting better.

The diagram opposite shows what happens when you feel under threat or in the grip of fear.

If you are able to *challenge* your 'Safety Behaviour' you can face the fear, as the diagram below shows.

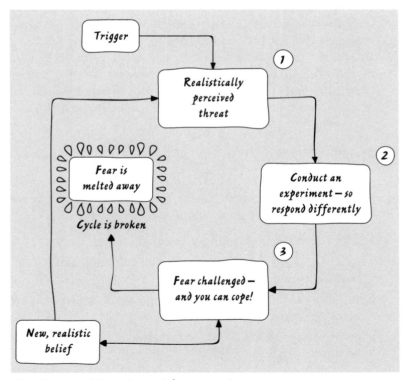

*Meeting a problem through 'exposure'*

If you break the fear cycle you can learn to cope. The fear melts away, like Suzi learning that a red face is not the worst thing in the world, so that she is gradually able to go out again.

## Reviewing the formulation

You need to be able to work out what has happened once you have stopped any 'Safety Behaviour'. Thus, if you have experimented with your problem, you need to take time to review your progress. How did it go? Did it work? How did you feel? Were your NATs not as accurate as you thought they were and did you do better than you expected?

You need to assess your progress and develop the next part of your self-experiment. This is called reviewing the formulation – it's a kind of rejigging of the blueprint in the light of the results you now have from your experiments. This way, you can chart your progress, see how far you have come, and work out if you are still moving towards your end goal. Notice if your NATs are changing too. Your old preoccupations may melt away as the fear melts. Continue with your Thought Record to map how you are changing, and continue to change your experiments accordingly.

## Chapter review

Just before you 'boldly go' on to the next chapter and beyond, like Spock, it's important to take a minute to recap what we have covered in this chapter. We have looked at how CBT:

- asks you to approach your problems scientifically;
- creates a 'blueprint' or 'formulation' of your problems, so you can 'see' them for yourself;
- suggests you test out your problems by identifying your 'Safety Behaviours' that are probably maintaining your problems;
- helps you to analyse which behaviours are maintaining your negative thoughts and feelings, and which negative thoughts and emotions are creating your behaviours.

**Your CBT change toolkit**

Tool no. 1: Make and stick with your decision to change.

Tool no. 2: Understand how you interpret the world and how you 'tick'.

Tool no. 3: Notice and note down negative thoughts.

Tool no. 4: Track down and eliminate your thinking errors

**Tool no. 5: Clarify problems and conduct experiments.**

The next few chapters will be applying what we have learned in the first five chapters to specific types of everyday problems. As human beings one of the most generic difficulties that we all share, in varying degrees, is issues to do with fear, anxiety and phobias.

**Homework**

Your very own Spock-like experimental chart

Think what you want to test out – keep it quite limited and defined and fill in this chart as you conduct your experiment.

| Prediction or theory | Experiment | Results | Conclusions |
|---|---|---|---|
| Outline the thought or belief you are testing. Rate its strength 0–100%. | Plan what you will do: the what, who, how, when, where, with whom. Be specific. | Record what actually happened: relevant thoughts, feelings, emotions, sensations, other people's reactions. | Write down what you have learned in light of results. Re-rate belief's strength 0–100%. |

**Chapter**

'Action may not always bring happiness; but there is no happiness without action.'

Benjamin Disraeli

# The 'Change Your Life with CBT' Plan: a reminder

A lot of information has been packed into Chapters 1–5, much of which might have been new to you. This brief chapter is here to help you recap:

- what you have learned so far;
- any things you may need to go back over;
- your decision to change;
- what you have decided to change;
- to help you consider your 'formulation' or 'blueprint' of your problems;
- whether you are currently on track with tackling them.

Hopefully, you will be making regular notes about your decision, your progress and your developments.

## CBT revision

You may find it helpful to refresh yourself at this point about the things you need to be doing to get a grip on your difficulties:

1. Keep a regular Thought Record (see p. 61).

---

**Change checker**

Tracking your NATs

How's it going with your Thought Record? Are you managing to keep one? If not, why not start today? Right now? If you are, how is it helping you focus?

---

2. This is your primary tool for catching your **negative automatic thoughts**, rather like having a large butterfly net to hand, to catch the winged specimens as they flutter by.

---

### Change checker

**Noticing your Dysfunctional Assumptions**

Have you noticed what your NATs tend to be about? Are there 'clusters' of NATs around particular issues? If you can spot any themes or regular issues, this will be helpful as you move on to the second half of this book, which is more about specifics such as anxiety, phobias, traumas, anger, etc. Have you noticed any obsessive thoughts? If so, Chapter 6 will be helpful.

Jot down what you think your NATs tend to be about.

---

Your **NATs** will give you an entry into where your problems come from. So you need to continue to do the **downward arrow process** – and follow your **NATs** through the **dysfunctional assumptions** to the **core beliefs** at the bottom (remember the glass: froth on top, liquid in the middle, sediment at the bottom).

---

### Change checker

**Identifying your Core Beliefs**

Take one or two of your most common NATs, and do a quick downward arrow process, so you can remind yourself of what your dysfunctional assumptions and Core Beliefs are. Use the following as an example.

---

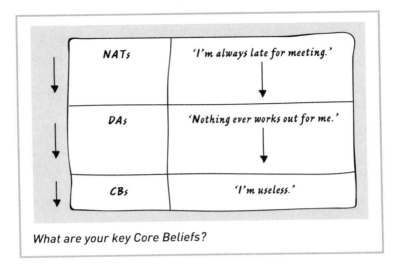

What are your key Core Beliefs?

3. Looking at your NATs and Thought Record – can you begin to identify any **thinking errors?** In Chapter 4, we looked in detail at the kinds of thinking errors you may be falling into. (Remember, a thinking error is a way of thinking that pervades your life, and which you can 'correct' if you start applying CBT principles – such as testing out how valid they are.) We identified the most common thinking errors as being the following:

- **black and white thinking** – the all or nothing perspective;
- **overgeneralising** – colouring everything the same;
- **mental filtering** – only seeing the bad, ignoring the good;
- **disqualifying the positive** – being a half-empty, rather than half-full thinker;
- **mind reading/fortune telling** – thinking you know what's real without really knowing;
- **magnifying and minimising** – being either a catastrophiser or denier, both of which can land you in trouble;

- **emotional reasoning** – working things out from feelings rather than thinking, also often known as 'magical thinking';
- **making 'should' statements** – always being beholden to 'should', 'ought' and 'must';
- **personalising** – seeing everything in personal terms, not being objective.

---

**Change checker**

**Teasing out your thinking errors**

What do you think your key thinking errors are?

---

4. We then moved on to making a blueprint or formulation of your problems (Chapter 5).

---

**Change checker**

**Formulating your problems**

Can you recall your formulation or blueprint? Can you do a quick sketch of how it works using a common NAT that occurs to you?

---

5. We also saw that we can **maintain** our difficulties in life (Chapter 5) through **Safety Behaviours** such as **aviodance**.

6. Do you have an idea of things you do or think that maintain your problems? Have you noticed your own particular Safety Behaviours concerning your issues? If so, make a note of them.

7. We also saw in Chapter 5 the importance of conducting **experiments** to start challenging our problems. The CBT way is to continue to do this, and keep revising your **formulation** – the **blueprint** of your problems – until your behaviour, or thoughts or emotions, begin to change.

8. This is usually done by **exposure** to something that is causing you anxiety, fear or another difficulty. You can start exposing yourself to something slowly, and on a small scale, until you build up to something more major or challenging. All the time you need to be monitoring your emotional reaction, and checking your anxiety levels.

---

### Change checker

**Conducting experiments on yourself**

Have you managed to conduct any experiments on yourself, to test your problems out? If so, what have you found out so far about yourself? What has worked? What has not worked?

---

9. If you have found using this book difficult, or have found any parts of CBT hard to understand so far, what is not clear? Jot down what you need to go over, or go back and revise by looking at the chapter again.

10. If you are ready to carry on, you can go to the next chapters according to what you are interested in ... or you can dip in and out, or read them sequentially. You will be building your knowledge of CBT throughout and, hopefully, building a picture of your own problems and how to change them.

## Important reminder

Things only change if:

- you want them to
- you do something about it yourself
- you make an effort to pinpoint what you want to change
- you make a plan and keep to it
- you try and stick to the suggestions in this book to make progress.

At this point you might be thinking that you need some extra help, a bit of hand holding, to help you on your way (some people find going to a therapist is a great step forward). If so, contact www.babcp.co.uk where you can find a CBT therapist or group.

Meanwhile, we are moving on now to four more chapters focused on specific issues:

- anxiety, phobias and obsessions
- depression
- anger.

CBT is not always easy to grasp at first, but the cumulative effect can be amazingly effective. Keep on going to get the best results.

Don't give up, keep moving forwards. Hang in there and your life will start to change. You're on your way to making your whole life better.

---

**Your CBT change toolkit**

Tool no. 1: Make and stick with your decision to change.

Tool no. 2: Understand how you interpret the world and how you 'tick'.

Tool no. 3: Notice and note down negative thoughts.

Tool no. 4: Track down and eliminate your thinking errors.

Tool no. 5: Clarify problems and conduct experiments.

**Tool no. 6: Review your decision, and keep deciding to change.**

---

Part

2

# How to use CBT to make your life better

Chapter

7

'It is not because things are difficult that
we do not dare: it is because we do not dare
that they are difficult.'

Seneca

# Riding the tiger: overcoming anxiety, panic, trauma, phobias and obsessions

In the first part of this book we looked at what exactly CBT is, how it works, and how it approaches your problems. The aim of CBT is to help you think, behave and feel more positively by helping you face the very fears or problems that you might want to escape from or avoid. As we have already seen, this can be done quite systematically and regularly and great results can be achieved relatively quickly.

In this second part of the book, we are going to look at particular areas of life that can cause us all a great deal of difficulty. A major strength of CBT work is that it is based on the notion of a *partnership* between the client (you) and the therapist (in the case of this book, me). We are both human, both fallible, and are probably both struggling with similar, human difficulties.

As a consequence, there is no 'us' and 'them' in CBT, rather we are both working towards finding a solution to something that is causing you grief. As this is a self-help book, the idea is that you will use it to help yourself work things out, just as if we were meeting for regular CBT sessions. So there will be a continuing emphasis on you applying any insights you may gain here to your own emotional life, and to being as systematic as you can be.

We are now going to look more specifically at the things that may well be holding you back in life: namely anxiety, panic, trauma, phobias and obsessions. Don't let the list put you off. All of these emotions are based on fear, at root. It is both possible, and desirable, to get a handle on these strong feelings, by learning to handle your fear constructively with CBT.

# What is fear for?

## Hard-wired humans

It's generally believed by researchers and others that feeling fear is hard-wired into us as human beings. After all, we need a certain level of fear to survive. Fear has a purpose: it is part of the primitive 'flight, fight or freeze' mechanism that we have evolved to survive in the wild and the world. We experience fear through our autonomous and central nervous systems, and it helps us preserve ourselves when we are in danger. The hard-wired response to attack means we will react before we can think, thus:

1. **Flight** – run away, avoid, escape;
2. **Fight** – turn and face a challenge, ready to attack or defend;
3. **Freeze** – be physically or mentally immobilised.

## Primitive responses to fear

If you are threatened or feel under attack, your mind and body will suddenly go into overdrive to work out how to tackle the situation effectively. Quite automatically, you start breathing rapidly, to get more oxygen to the brain, so you can think better: you need all your wits about you to face the challenge. People who are in accidents can often remember the exact moment when it happened and describe everything slowing down, just like 'slow-mo' in a film.

Our experiences of time, and our senses of smell, taste, touch, sound, sight, can all be distorted and recorded, literally etched on to our memories, in the few seconds when we are under threat. This is because the brain becomes instantly sharper and more focused, fuelled by life-saving biochemicals, governed by the *amygdala* (in the limbic nervous system), a centre of raw emotion and response, deep in the brain, which makes us notice everything in fine detail, fuelled by our fear.

As the heart beats faster, and we breathe more rapidly, fresh, oxygen-rich blood gets to our muscles, priming us to 'flight or fight'. Or, if the fears or threats are simply too enormous and overwhelming, or we perceive we can't easily escape, we may 'freeze' to save ourselves. Meanwhile, adrenalin and cortisol start pumping into the blood stream, as well as the oxygenated blood, and the sweat glands become more active (to cool the body if it is overheating from trying to 'escape').

Then, blood is drained from the skin towards the heart, as the whole body goes into a state of 'red alert' to act rapidly (which is why people look so pale when under threat). All of this happens automatically, instantaneously, and can lead to feelings of light-headedness, dizziness, trembling hands, knees, fingers, feet, pins and needles, breathlessness and feelings of being unreal.

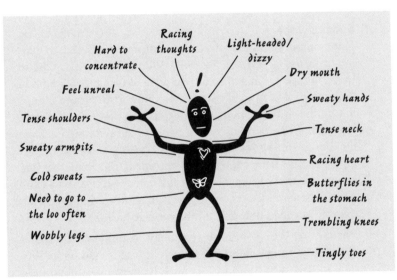

*Reacting to threat or challenge*

## The coping reaction

Our 'anxiety response' of 'flight, fight or freeze' happens so instantaneously, and so unbidden, that we have no time to actually *think* about what is happening. We just react. And it's an autonomous reaction, leading to further motor reactions and usually completely beyond any conscious control. All this pumping of oxygen, blood, adrenalin and cortisol makes us primed and the *'coping reaction'* takes over. Muscles are tense, we are more alert, we respond more quickly, our brains race, our palms sweat as we are pushed to work out how to survive.

---

Miranda was walking casually along the pavement one fine spring afternoon, pushing Jemima, her toddler, strapped happily into her new buggy. Jemima had just nodded off to sleep, and Miranda was enjoying a rare moment of peace, window shopping, working out what to buy for supper, and saying 'Hi' to friends and neighbours as she strolled down the high street of her rural home town.

Suddenly she was horribly aware of an enormous, black, shiny object mounting the pavement, roaring loudly, rushing towards herself and her child. With absolutely no time to think, Miranda realised a car had gone out of control and was heading directly for her and, more importantly, the sleeping Jemima in her buggy. With gigantic power, a strength she had never found before in her life, Miranda instinctively picked up the buggy and hurled it sideways, diving rugby-try style after it through a shop entrance, smashing the side window. Luckily the car veered further down the street and finally came to a screeching halt, buried in another shop window (no one but the drunk-driver was harmed).

Recounting the event later, an uncontrollably shaking and shocked Miranda could not believe that she had been able to find the superhuman strength to pick the child-laden buggy up (she found it very hard to lift her daughter in it usually), or the wherewithal to calculate the space between herself and the shop doorway.

It had all happened in a split second, and Miranda was amazed, although obviously grateful, that her quick thinking and acting had saved the life of herself and her daughter. Although they were both badly cut, bruised and shocked, Miranda's autonomic and instinctive 'flight' anxiety response and coping reaction had thankfully saved both their lives.

---

---

**Test yourself**

**Your flight, fight or freeze reactions**

Can you remember a time when you reacted quickly in an emergency, or when under threat? What happened? How did you feel? Could you recall the situation clearly afterwards, and if so, what happened?

---

## The trouble with long-term anxiety

Miranda's 'primitive response' is immediate, and her fear reactions appropriate. But sometimes our fears take over, in everyday life, and leave us feeling jittery, anxious, tense, for no apparent or obvious reason. This kind of enduring anxiety is unhealthy, and can cause all sorts of psychological, behavioural and physical problems if left unchecked.

The issue is, if you are primed for emergencies, on red alert all the time, your stomach will fill with acid (which is why people get ulcers), and your brain and body will be full of all sorts of biochemicals (such as adrenalin and cortisol), and excess blood supply, leading to migraines, tension headaches, even strokes and heart attacks. So you really need to get a handle on prolonged anxiety, when you are away from immediate, real threat. To do that, we need to understand where anxiety actually comes from in more detail.

# Where does anxiety come from?

While fear is a primitive emotion, anxiety is like a 'spin-off' feeling of tension and jitteryness, which can be short lived, or turned on fairly long term.

## Hereditary factors

Can anxiety be inherited? Is there a genetic link? It's estimated now by researchers that there could be a significant genetic link in certain types of fear and anxiety. This link has been established through studies of twins with the same genetic make-up, who end up being twice as likely as the general population to have the same kinds of anxiety and fear.

Also, a specific gene (the 17th out of the 23 we all have), called the *SERT* (serotonin transfer gene), has been identified as having a connection to *anxiety disorders*. Scientists think people with what is called a 'short' form of the gene may be prone to anxiety and depression, unlike people with a 'long' form of the gene (despite any adverse childhood circumstances).

Also it seems also that your *general personality type* has something to do with how anxious you are: so someone who is sensitive, volatile, reactive, excitable, highly strung, a worry-wort, may be more prone to anxiety attacks than someone who is more docile, unexcitable, ruminative or level-headed.

## Childhood factors

Although CBT is very focused on the 'here and now' it's worth just mentioning that childhood factors may well contribute towards your being more anxious, phobic, and generally fearful. It might seem obvious, but researchers have found that people brought up in the following circumstances might well end up being more anxious generally. Their parents may well have been:

- overly critical of them, making them reach high or impossible standards;
- emotionally repressive or punitive;
- physically repressive (using corporal punishment);
- highly anxious themselves – communicating the world 'out there' is a dangerous place;
- emotionally unstable or addicted/dependent themselves;
- abusive on an emotional, physical or sexual level;
- seriously overprotective.

Megan is a very overprotective mother. She worries all the time about the traffic, and won't let her child out of the house past the front gate. This was fine while her son was young, but now he is 11 and starting secondary school she insists on wanting to go with him. *'You don't know the traffic as I do'*, says Megan anxiously to James. *'You might cross the road without looking, and then you'll be hit by a car.'* Megan is clearly a highly anxious person, who doesn't have much practical or financial support, so she perceives danger everywhere all the time: even if it's not actually apparent in the moment.

The problem with Megan's overprotectiveness is that not only does she keep herself in a constant state of anxiety and red alert, which causes undue wear and tear on her, physically and emotionally. But it also has an effect on her son, in the short and longer term.

Not helping him to trust himself on the road, or use his wits, means that he will actually become 'disabled' in the outside world. It will actually make him more, rather than less vulnerable, as he will feel a huge lack of confidence in himself as he crosses the road. Ironically, Megan is in danger of transferring her anxiety on to her son's shoulders so that he, in turn, will fear street life unduly.

Yes, of course he will have to learn to cross the road, but he will also need to find his way, deal with people, become streetwise and learn these things by himself, to gain self-confidence and go on his way in life. Also, in time, he could even become secretive and resentful towards his mother, by not letting her know what he gets up to because he fears her overprotective overreaction. So, all round, it would be better for Megan to learn to conquer her anxiety and help her son to trust himself in the world.

## Stress factors

When you are feeling stressed you are more vulnerable to feeling anxiety and fear, and flipping into panic. So it's important to take action if you are feeling increasingly stressed. Check out the list below. Are any of these situations similar to something you are going through?

---

**Reality check**

Modern life's top stress points

- divorce and separation
- death or illness of a close family member
- moving house (especially older people)
- getting fired (also threat of redundancy)
- domestic strife
- injury and/or illness (including chronic illness)
- pregnancy
- getting married
- bankruptcy
- redundancy and job loss
- starting a new job (and doing multiple jobs)
- having a baby
- arrest and going to prison.

---

**Test yourself**

Understanding your own stress points

Is there anything happening in your life right now that might be causing stress? Are you experiencing any of the stress points listed above, or have you experienced any of them in the past six months? Take a moment to jot them down. What's been pushing your buttons on the stress front recently? Are you feeling more anxious or reactive than usual as a consequence? If so, how?

---

# Understanding 'healthy' anxiety

It is essential to have a certain level of fear and anxiety in your life – otherwise you simply wouldn't survive. This chapter is not going to tell you how to eliminate all these primitive, instinctual feelings. You'd end up a zombie without them, or completely vulnerable and unreal. Rather it is going to explain how you can use these 'hard-wired' emotions to a better end.

Feelings of anxiety can actually become something you no longer dread, or run from, and become instead something you can accept as part of being human. At the same time, if your fear and anxiety are overwhelming, it's important to be able to get a handle on them, so you can go about your everyday life as fruitfully as possible.

Graham, a 33-year-old actor, explains that whenever he goes on stage, or on TV, he has terrible butterflies. He can't sleep the night before, he wakes up with a headache, he feels sick and dry mouthed, but he's learned that it's all part of the necessary preparation for a performance. The only problem on his mind is whether he will 'corpse' and forget his lines completely: something that happened once when he was at drama school. *'I've learned not to drink anything the night before a show, as I know it will knock out my brain cells', says Graham with a laugh. 'Anyway, the stage fright is all part of giving a good performance, I've now found – so I use them to give my acting an edge.'*

## Be aware of your feelings

Be aware that as you read this chapter about anxiety, fear, trauma, phobias and so on it may well bring up the very feelings you might be trying to avoid. You might feel fear exactly because the book seems too accurate, or it reflects or stirs up your feelings too much.

Like putting your finger in the flame, it may make you feel a panicky: *'What's wrong with me?'* or *'OhMyGod, I've got real problems. I'm in serious trouble.'* Stop there. Don't panic (no, really, don't panic). You are a human being, so it is completely normal to feel some level of fear – even unbidden. Don't be hard on yourself as a consequence. Try to ride the tiger, so you can stay on track and get the most out of this book.

**Remember, fear and anxiety are:**

- **completely normal emotions**, so we all experience them from time to time;
- **time limited**, although, when you feel them intensely, at that time you probably think they will go on forever;
- **helping you survive** and function, so you don't want to eliminate them completely, but nor do you want to be swamped by them;
- **a signal** that something is happening – but you can learn to read the signals so you know what to do.

## Fear of fear itself

If you are suffering from 'anxiety' you may well be experiencing heightened feelings of fear most of the time. This will often be accompanied by 'extreme thinking', where you describe or think about things regularly with words such as 'horrific', 'terrible', 'horrible', 'ghastly', 'scary', 'dreadful' and 'awful'.

The 'thinking errors' you will be experiencing are of the 'catastrophising', 'black and white' and 'filtering' kind (we met thinking errors in Chapter 4), where the slightest thing can seem to be hailing the end of the world. This is not to belittle the condition one bit, but is to show that when fear becomes the fear itself it becomes quite hard for you to discriminate between real and perceived threat.

---

**Insight**

Obsessive compulsive disorder occurs when your fear is so overwhelming that you try to fend it off with rituals or compulsions. It's a way of trying to keep the overpowering feelings of anxiety at bay, and can take the following forms:

---

- counting numbers, making lists
- checking things repeatedly
- washing hands, washing objects
- putting things in order, alphabetical, or colour-coded
- being preoccupied with particular words, thoughts, phrases
- swearing, being lewd or shouting excessively (also called Tourette's Syndrome).

## How to tame your tiger

The first issue to deal with when trying to tame your fear and anxiety is to understand what triggers you off from a CBT perspective. This book is necessarily focused on trying to help you to help yourself, so you need to become aware of whatever makes you vulnerable, or whatever NATs pop up as a warning sign. We're going to look now at different scenarios and work out how your fears could be healthily defused.

## Understanding your anxiety

### How do I know when I'm anxious?

First, check for symptoms: if you are heading into any kind of anxiety attack, you will probably get some, if not all, of the following symptoms:

- feeling restless (twitchy arms, legs, facial twitches)
- difficulty concentrating
- sweaty hands, head, neck, etc.
- muscle tension (neck, headaches)
- difficulties sleeping (slow to fall asleep, waking up in the night)
- irritability, snappiness
- stomach tension, 'butterflies', indigestion
- desire to blank out feelings with alcohol or drugs

- desire to numb out with cigarettes, drugs, TV, computer games, etc.
- feeling fatigued for no 'real' reason
- loss of appetite/overeating.

**"**Everything is so dangerous that nothing is really very frightening.**"**
Gertrude Stein

| 'Normal' anxiety | Anxiety disorders |
|---|---|
| Real sense of threat ⟶ | Extreme sense of threat<br>Excessive worry<br>Overestimation of dire consequences<br>Rumination, inflexible thinking, inability to cope |
| Reasonable ⟶<br>apprehension/worry | Extreme worry<br>Fear of going 'mad'<br>Terror of losing control, going OTT, dying |
| Exaggerated thinking ⟶<br>linked to threat<br>(short-lived) | Constant 'catastrophising'<br>'All or nothing' thinking all the time (long term)<br>Permanent exaggerated thinking |
| Physical responses<br>to anxiety | Physical responses re anxiety disorders |
| Racing heart ⟶ | Constant palpitations |
| Muscle tension ⟶ | Chest pains, exhaustion, muscle pain, headaches |
| Fast breathing ⟶ | Panting, dizziness, feeling unreal |
| Tense stomach ⟶<br>'butterflies' | Nausea, needing to go to the toilet all the time, diarrhoea |
| Increased ⟶<br>sweating | Extreme sweating |
| Blood drains ⟶<br>from head to<br>heart | Skin problems, fainting, blotchy skin |

*How anxiety can become chronic*

# The kinds of anxiety you can experience

The main issue with your anxiety is the intensity and level it is at. Try to work out exactly how anxious you are using your Thought Record. Estimate its intensity, say from 0–100 percent. Think about what kind of anxiety you have from the following descriptions.

## Anxiety vs. anxiety disorder

Anxiety is an inevitable part of modern life. Anxiety can occur in different forms and at different levels of intensity, according to the situation, your personality, the circumstances, your personal history, and your own personal psychology and heredity. You can experience anything from a twinge of discomfort to a full-blown panic attack. It might be in response to a particular thing, or might descend on you, *'out of the blue'*. This latter type of anxiety is called *'free-floating anxiety'* and can pop up seemingly unannounced (for example, you suddenly feel nervous, but you don't know why).

If your anxiety is actually attached to something tangible it might be what is called *'situational anxiety'* or *'phobic anxiety'*, as the feelings of fear are attached to something specific. Worrying unduly about something that might happen in the future is called *'anticipatory anxiety'*. (Say, when you are going to meet your partner's parents for the first time, and you're sure you'll mess it up, say the wrong thing, fall over Woody Allen-style).

The following are the kinds of anxiety feelings you might experience:

- shaking and trembling
- tearfulness
- tight feeling in the chest
- nausea or tummy cramps
- light-headedness or dizziness
- feeling unreal
- fear you will die

- choking or a 'lump in the throat' feeling
- fear you will 'go crazy' or get out of control
- hot flushes or sudden chills
- numbness or tingling limbs
- feeling of unreality, of being detached
- racing heart, irregular heartbeat
- breathlessness, feeling unable to get any air
- sweating.

> Mary sits at her desk needing to make a phone call to a buyer, but she can't bear to pick up the phone. Her hand shakes as it hovers over the receiver. Recently she has had the feeling of having something stuck in her throat, as big as an apricot stone, every time she has to make a call. Then she needs to go to the loo before she calls, and she spends time putting on lipstick, or wandering to the water cooler, or making yet more coffee. Indeed she'd rather do anything than make that call. The last time she spoke to the buyer he sneered at her and lost his temper, and she felt really put down and humiliated. Now her boss is leaning on her to make more sales – with this particular buyer – before the end of the month. Mary sneaks off for an early lunch – she still hasn't made the call – and now has 'one of her headaches'. She heads for the pub, where she intends to get some Dutch courage over a liquid lunch. Mary knows, deep down, that she is digging herself a deeper hole by avoiding the call, but her fear has taken over.

In extreme cases this kind of anxiety can become an *'anxiety disorder'* if it becomes so intense, or so prolonged, that it interferes with your everyday life to a serious degree. An anxiety disorder is where the panic button has been pressed and stays on, not just for a few minutes until the emergency (or perceived emergency) has passed, but for hours, days, weeks, months, even years. And it can severely affect your health if it is not dealt with effectively.

## See your GP

If this is true of you, and if your anxiety symptoms persist *for at least a week* you'll need to get medical help and talk to your GP. There is a diagnostic test your GP can use to help work out just how anxious you are. Don't worry, this doesn't necessarily lead to medication, but it might well lead to you getting some practical help on the NHS, including seeing a CBT therapist. The longer you leave your anxiety symptoms – undiagnosed and unchallenged – the longer they are going to persist.

To help you further identify your anxiety for yourself, here are some other common types of fear.

## Social anxiety

This is also known as 'social phobia' and includes such things as fear of meeting people, social situations, talking in public, being looked at, performing, even eating or drinking, or simply being seen, in public.

- **Gary** has been told to present a report to the sales meeting, but he is utterly terrified of speaking in front of people, especially his boss. He feels too shy and self-conscious standing up in front of them, and knows he will mess up the PowerPoint – it's a scene from his worst nightmare.

- **Sophie** finds it increasingly difficult to go to the shops on a Saturday, because she feels fearful of walking into a busy clothing shop and being stared at critically, or having to take her clothes off in a communal dressing room.

- **Shamir** screens his phone calls and feels very shy and self-conscious if he picks up the phone, and finds himself caught off guard. He doesn't know what to say, especially if he is put on the spot. He also finds it hard to say 'No' when 'cold callers' pressure him on the phone.

- **Marie** bought a jumper in a big department store, but when she got home she found it had a thread unravelling and missing buttons. However, she is unable to return it, even though she has the receipt and tags, because she feels it would be impossible to confront the sales people.

- **Barry** gets invited out to the local day centre, as he lives alone, but he is worried about other people seeing him eat. He feels self-conscious about his weight, and would rather stay in, and eat alone.

## Health anxiety

This can include fear of dying, injury or of contracting a life-threatening disease.

- **Simon** finds himself worrying a great deal when he finds any lumps and bumps on his body and is always lying awake at night thinking he is dying of something awful. He goes to the doctor to check them out frequently – they are nearly always nothing.

- **Katrina** often lies awake at night worrying she will die too soon, before her son has grown up and is able to live an independent life without her.

- **Sandy** washes his hands every ten minutes or so throughout the day, and even gets up at night to do so, and scrubs his hands with a nailbrush. He is horrified by dirt, and sprays everything with antibacterial spray. He even has plastic on his chairs, as he is terrified of getting a horrible disease.

# Handling an anxiety attack effectively

Let's take a situation where anxiety has reached a high level – what can you actually do?

Don, 31, a lawyer, is lying in bed. His marriage has recently ended, and it's been a messy, stressful divorce. It's 3 in the morning and he can't sleep. As he lies there, his mind races, and he begins to feel a sense of dread. Thoughts start floating up: *'I'm horribly alone'*, *'I'm going to die, and no one will be here to help me'* and *'my life's nearly over, I'll never fall in love again.'*

As these NATs surface Don feels his jaw and stomach clench, his mouth goes dry and he feels sick and tearful. Suddenly everything and everyone feels far away; he feels unreal and remote.

What can Don do to quell the anxiety? If you ever feel like him at all, you can:

- Put the light on and sit up. Changing the situation can help to deal with rising fear. If you can't sleep, anxiety will worsen while you lie there, fretting. Get up and make yourself a warm milky drink (no alcohol, no nicotine or caffeine).

- Accept the feelings, don't push them away. Trying to deny or flatten the feelings will actually accentuate them. You need to tell yourself something like, *'I'm feeling scared at the moment, but that's completely OK, it's natural in this situation – it will pass'*.

- Sit up and write down all the NATs in your Thought Record. Note every last thing down about all your fears. Keep a pad and pen by the bed, and even a little torch, if you don't want to wake up a partner, so you can write in the dark.

- Make a list of every single worry, every perplexing problem, and then fold up the list and put it under your pillow for the morning.

- Remember that you've been here before – and you've lived. You've probably experienced all of this in the past, and probably worse, and it hasn't killed you. This moment of anxiety will pass, as all things do. Even thought it feels like it will go on forever, it will subside.

- If you are scared by something specific, you will need to take yourself away from the situation and put your attention on something else briefly, such as listening to some soothing classical music, or the radio, or looking at the stars out of the window. Even counting to ten can help. And looking at something in detail, say a picture, or stroking a pet or reading a book, can help calm you.

Other simple things you can do if anxiety hits are:

- simple relaxation techniques
- easy meditation.

You can turn to either of the exercises described below the minute you feel anxiety symptoms creeping up your back. I find myself thinking, 'Oh here we go again' when particular thoughts or symptoms occur. Using my CBT knowledge, I can see the anxious thoughts are repetitive and reminding me I feel worried or frightened. I can then do something, such as relax or meditate, to steer myself on to a calmer path.

You can do these exercises at work, in your lunch break, at a local park, in the car park or even the loo, at home, at school, at an airport, in the car, at a traffic jam, on a train, in the garden, in bed – wherever you find yourself beginning to feel overcome by fearful feelings.

## A simple relaxation technique

Relaxation. What a word. So easy to say, so hard to do. 'Relax' we say to each other, 'enjoy yourself. It might never happen'. Well, if you're anxious, you feel it will happen, any minute, so you have to be vigilant 24/7. The thing is, learning to relax is really a great way to start unravelling the threads that keep us totally wound up. Like Don above, you may feel you can't sleep at night, and lie there fretting, hoping that you can sleep, but fearing that you won't drop off – and then everything will be helter-skelter the next day. Panic rises as you begin to feel you can't cope, so your heart rate begins to race, you feel restless, sweaty, scared.

Good news: most GPs and therapists will now help you to learn some simple relaxation techniques as a way of dealing with all sorts of anxiety.

## How to relax

1. Lie or sit with your eyes closed. Make sure you are warm and comfortable, with no restrictive clothes and no draughts or distractions.
2. Take a deep breath in, and then out.
3. Notice your breath as it comes in naturally, then let it go.
4. Start by thinking of your toes, focus on them. Tense them, and relax them.

5. Keep breathing slowly and evenly, noticing your breath, and letting it go. You might like to do this a couple of times.
6. Then move on to your ankles, flex or rotate them, and relax them. Feel them heavy, leaden, sinking into the floor.
7. Then move up to your calves, your knees, thighs, hips and upwards, through each part of your body, bit by bit.
8. Until you get to your jaw, your head, eyes, neck, brow. All the time, breathe slowly and deeply, noticing your breathing.

Then just let yourself sink into the floor, the bed, the chair. And after a few minutes you can open your eyes.

## Other quick stress busters

For simple techniques that you can use, say at your desk, try the following.

### The shoulder shrug

1. Stop working, stand up.
2. Lift your shoulders up to your ears, squeeze them, really hard, and then drop them.
3. Do this three times.
4. Then stretch as high as you can towards the ceiling, then shake out the tension in your hands and feet, just like a swimmer before a race.

### And

### The hold 'em high stretch

1. Stand up, raise your arms up to the ceiling – stretch.
2. Bring your arms slowly down to your sides.
3. Flex your jaw, and open your mouth wide and yawn, like a goldfish. Do this three times in a row.
4. Raise your arms again above your head, and go up on tip toes, to stretch your back.
5. Jiggle your shoulders and hands to shake out the fear.

## Easy meditation

Meditation is one of those things that always sounds very fancy and fandangled, but actually is amazingly easy to do and effective to use. I do it every day, for 15 minutes, and the whole day goes better as a consequence. I especially do it when I feel panicky about time, and about getting things done, when I feel *'I haven't got time'*. Meditation seems to stretch time, and ease fear, so it is brilliant with any kind of anxiety.

### Five-minute meditation: a taster

1. Find a quiet spot in the house, garden or somewhere you feel safe.

2. Put on a timer for five minutes.

3. Sit comfortably in a chair or on a bed, or even lie down (you don't have to be cross legged in a lotus position, but it helps).

4. Close your eyes.

5. As you breathe in think 'rising'.

6. As you breathe out think 'falling'.

7. That's all you do. Keep doing this, rising and falling, as you breathe in and out.

8. As all the NATs and worrisome thoughts float across your mind – *'Did I put the oven off?'* or *'What time is it?'* – let them go, bring your attention back to your breath and settling your attention to the spot between your eyes, behind your brows.

9. Keep refocusing your attention as you breathe in and out, and don't scratch an itch, open your eyes or get distracted, even if the phone rings. Ignore it and just keep breathing and refocusing behind your mid-brow until your timer goes off.

10. Slowly open your eyes. Then get up slowly and stretch. You'll feel refreshed, calm and your anxiety levels will probably have dropped.

As you get used to meditating you can stretch the time to 10 minutes, then 15 or 20. You can also do it night and morning, or in the middle of the day, or all three. Also, you can do it in the middle of the night in bed (without a timer) if your mind is racing and you can't relax enough to sleep.

### Meditation marvel

The great thing about meditation is that it slows down the alpha rhythms in the brain, so that your mind is actually in a kind of 'suspended animation'. A great story about the famous French Buddhist monk, Matthieu Ricard (who is also a PhD in biology and a research scientist) is told in his wonderful book, *Happiness: A Guide to Developing Life's Most Important Skill* [Atlantic Books, London, 2007]). He has meditated daily for 35 years and seems to be the happiest, calmest, most delightful person anyone could meet.

As part of an experiment to test him out, he was put into an MRI scanner for three hours to see how his brain works. Most people find the MRI experience daunting and uncomfortable, even for a short time. However, when he emerged from the noisy, confined machine, he was smiling and said simply 'that was like a mini retreat'. Such is the power of meditation and the controlled mind.

However, Benny, 29, hates going on the London Underground. He gets a real feeling of panic every time he goes down the escalator, into the hot bowels of the earth. There's something about being closed in a train that sets his pulse racing, makes him breathless and dizzy and increasingly, recently, he has had a fear that the train will stop in a tunnel and he'll get stuck underground for hours. 'I think I read a lot of reports about the attacks on 7/7 and that got to me,' explains Benny. *'Now, if the train halts for more than a minute, I can feel my heart starting to pound and I start looking round panicking, searching for an escape.'*

> Benny is clearly feeling major panic, not only once he is in the train, but also as he goes down the escalator. Increasingly he says he is avoiding the Tube, and going by bus or even walking, so he doesn't have to go underground. The thing is, it's making him late for meetings and dates, and sometimes it is simply unavoidable to go by Tube when he has to be somewhere on time.

So what can Benny do? If, like him, you suffer from rising panic, what can you do to stop it becoming a full-blown panic attack?

Apart from the simple relaxation technique and easy meditation described above (both of which are helpful with panic attacks), there seems to be evidence that nipping an attack in the bud is very important.

Thus, at the very moment that you begin to sense you are feeling uncontrollably anxious, and are going to panic, with the hairs standing up on the back of your neck, or your stomach tightening, you will inevitably have some NATs surfacing, such as *'I've got to get out of here'* or *'help, let me out'*.

## Soothe the red alert with positive self-talk

At the precise moment, the early warning signals are there with the NATs so you need to watch out for your red alert. You need to consciously change the words rising in your mind from *'I've got to get out of here'*, to *'All is well, I'm fine, the train will move soon, there is nothing to worry about'*. You need to soothe your fear with positive self-talk. You need to tell yourself all is well, or you are fine, and talk yourself down – just as if someone else (a good friend, a parent, a therapist) were talking to you, calmly.

So if you were on the train, like Benny, with panic rising:

1.  Take a deep breath in, close your eyes.
2.  Say to yourself, *'all is well'*, or *'I am fine'* or *'I can cope with this'*.
3.  Say this to yourself over and over, as if it were a mantra.

4. Keep breathing slowly, calmly (don't breathe too deeply or you may hyperventilate, and make yourself worse).

5. You could also text a friend or spouse to tell them how you feel – that will relieve pressure.

6. You could talk to someone, even just to comment on how you feel, as talking about it, even briefly, can diffuse the panic – isolation usually makes it worse.

## Creative visualisation

In using creative visualisation techniques people imagine, in their mind's eye, that they are doing calming things such as strolling down a cool, leafy country lane, or walking by the sea and feeling the breeze in their hair. It is perfectly possible to do this anywhere, especially if you feel a panic attack coming on.

My own personal favourite is imagining a light, glittery purple curtain, like a sheer waterfall, creating a barrier between myself and the thing that is scaring me. I hate crowded trains, and it is precisely when I feel that panic rising on a hot summer's day, when I'm stuffed into an overcrowded carriage, that I can close my eyes and imagine a wonderful, shimmery sheen of purple cascading over me, like a wispy curtain. With practice, it works wonders, and makes me feel cool and collected.

Creative visualisation is often used with people who have life-threatening illnesses, such as cancer, or for dealing with difficult medical procedures. In a way it is linked to meditation, in that you can calm your mind down and let the alpha rhythms take over, as your pulse slows down, too.

## The paper bag trick

Alongside relaxation, meditation and creative visualisation, an old technique for panic is simply to breathe in and out of a paper bag. You seal the bag round your mouth with your hands, and breathe in and out a few times, counting up to ten. This works mainly on the level of distracting you away from panicky, shallow breathing, or panting, which can escalate an attack.

# Dealing with phobias

If you are phobic you will be afraid of an object (such as a spider) or a situation (say being in a lift) that evokes your fear reaction, and bodily symptoms (breathlessness, racing heart). Phobic fear is intense, immediate, and can attach to a wide range of things, such as animals, the environment (open spaces, i.e., agoraphobia), experiences (such as flying), blood (think *Doc Martin* on TV), foods, even vomit.

## Steps to handling your phobia

1. Accept in the first place that you have a phobia – don't deny it.

2. If you are confronted with something you hate – such as a daddy-long-legs or dog poo – then take a second, as the panic rises, to say *'I can deal with this'* to yourself. Positive affirmations or self-talk are very effective in dealing with panic.

3. If you know you can't deal with being in the same place as something like the daddy-long-legs, simply remove yourself. If you are trapped with it, such as being in a car, then it is important you think practically about driving the car to the side of the road, and parking, before getting out. Don't just give in to the panic if you can help it.

4. Get help – you may need a trusted friend or relative (or therapist) to help you familiarise yourself with the object of your fear. If it's a daddy-long-legs, ask them to put it in a sealed jar, so you can be in the same room. Test out how near you can be without panicking – make notes afterwards in your Thought Record. Note your fear levels at the outset of any 'experiments', and then note them again afterwards.

5. Set up a series of tests, at regular intervals, of you exposing yourself slowly to the object of fear – even a few seconds is better than nothing – so you can begin to desensitise yourself. Once you can exist in a room with a daddy-long-legs in the corner, without freaking out, then you have moved forwards hugely – congratulate yourself.

6. Keep exposing yourself *very* gradually and slowly to the daddy-long-legs, even to the point that you might eventually touch it with a glove on, or even pick it up.

7. Don't expose yourself too fast to the object of your fear – that can set you back. Take your time to prepare yourself, and try it little and often as a way of *desensitising* yourself to the thing you are afraid of.

8. Measure how far you have come towards normalising the situation by estimating your fear levels – first, before exposure, and second, afterwards. Keep a diary of your Thought Records throughout.

---

**Change checker**

Find your phobias

Have you got any phobias? Have you worked out if you have any new ones? Make a note for future reference.

---

# Dealing with trauma

## Post-traumatic stress disorder (or syndrome)

This disorder usually follows a life-threatening situation, such as an accident, being attacked or abused, experiencing a disaster or being at war, where the fear in the situation was enormous and you experienced pain, terror, or actually were totally out of control. Symptoms typically are of 'flashbacks' to the moment of threat or actual harm, nightmares and night sweats, an enduring sense of danger (hypervigilance), and being on edge, irritable, angry, ashamed, disgusted and reactive.

Sometimes memories are very clear about the event or situation, while at others they are fragmented, or hard to catch hold of, leaving a generalised feeling of threat. You can be pulled towards wanting to eradicate and avoid the feelings of discomfort with 'props' such as alcohol, drugs or sugar.

Anna was terrified of thunderstorms (tonitro-phobia), which reminded her of growing up in the former Yugoslavia during the troubles in the 1990s. Since then she has hidden away, under the sheets, even in a cupboard, as the fear of the thunder and lightening evoked raw terror. Her life had begun to 'shut down' in other ways too. She had started staying in and not seeing friends. Her unprocessed trauma was beginning to made her socially anxious and agoraphobic as well. Her husband said he couldn't stand it any more, as their life together had become isolated and ruled by her fear. Anna eventually went to her GP, who referred her for CBT. After ten sessions, where Anna began to confront her fears, she was able to stay in the living room, with her husband, when the thunderclouds rolled. Anna was gradually exposed to the noise, the flashes and her accompanying scary thoughts, in therapy. Over time she understood that the horrendous threats she had lived under as a child were now past. Thunder was now thunder, not a life-threatening war.

# The power of exposure

## Gradually facing your fears

As we saw in Chapter 5 and in the section above on phobias, CBT uses the technique of *gradual exposure* to the very things that you might find terrifying – be it public speaking, living alone, big dogs, being in a car – whatever it is that is holding you back. Say, like Anna, you are terrified of thunder storms:

1. You would need to note down what triggers your fear, then how you think you'll feel if you experienced it (*anticipated anxiety*).

2. Having exposed yourself to being caught in a storm (even for a few minutes), note how you really feel (*actual anxiety*). Thus:

Assessing Anna's 'tonitrophobia'

| Anxiety response trigger: | Anticipated anxiety levels | Actual anxiety levels |
|---|---|---|
| **On:** Hearing thunder Seeing storm clouds or darkening skies Seeing lightning flashes | On a scale of 0–100 (say 90%) | Exposure 60% |

# Dealing with obsessions

Whole books have been written on obsessions, obsessive compulsive disorder and addictions, so this is just to remind you that any obsessions will be based on extreme feelings of fear, a need for control, a desire for perfection. Often obsessions focus on the need for cleanliness, order, superb hygiene, as the real fear behind it is of dying, or getting ill, or being out of control.

Some people will become obsessed with objects, including other people (say stalkers, extreme fans), or things (such as collecting or hoarding things such as newspapers; or shoes). Or the obsession may be behavioural, such as counting numbers; collecting train, plane or automobile names; or putting things in order, such as pencils, books, papers or CDs. Some obsessional behaviours focus on checking things over and over, or even saying things repeatedly.

If you have OCD you may feel over-responsible, with a desire for unattainable perfection, and find it hard to tolerate things not being as you want them to be. Obsessive behaviour may also include avoiding things that make you feel uncomfortable (such as dirt or animals), or being preoccupied with your negative thoughts. To combat them, CBT will either suggest you:

- reduce or stop the ritual or behaviour or thoughts, and see how this affects your thoughts, behaviour and feelings; or
- increase your thoughts or behaviour, to see how this affects you.

Simon is obsessed with turning door handles to face upwards before he goes to sleep. He has done this since he was a child, and goes round the house at night turning the handles upwards, so that he feels more secure. His partner finds this behaviour increasingly annoying, since Simon becomes distressed and obsessed with whether he has done it or not. So he has to go round checking all over again. With CBT help he decided to stop, but first of all he experimented with doubling his efforts to turn up the handles, morning, noon and night, and noting his feelings and thoughts on his Thought Record. He began to see he was worrying about the ritual even more now he was checking more. His obsession with door handles was being exacerbated by his behaviour of checking them – the very opposite of what he thought would happen. So Simon decided to stop checking, and after 12 weeks of sessions he was able to go to bed checking them only once, much to the relief of his partner. His main goal, over time, was to give up checking altogether.

## Hold the hand washing

One client was obsessed with washing her hands before, during and after our sessions, and needed to keep doing it throughout the day and night. One way we tackled the obsession was to 'allow' her to wash her hands as many times as she wanted, until she became exhausted (and chapped). After this she found she began to want to limit her hand washing.

This is similar to the technique of telling someone not to think about the green bunny rabbit sitting on their head. They inevitably look up, above their head, to try to see the bunny rabbit sitting there. It is only human to want to do the very thing that you have been exhorted not to do. When you are obsessed it is your inner voice which is telling you to do the behaviour all the time, so you need to learn to outwit that voice.

## Dealing with addictions

Similarly with addictions. If you are eating compulsively, and you know precisely where the biscuits are, and what's in the fridge, you may find yourself trying hard not to go there, and then feel compelled to open the door, and eat. Again, you might find it useful to give yourself permission to do so, until you feel you have had enough. 'Having enough' is often difficult to gauge when you are acting addictively in any way. At the same time, to set yourself some realistic limits, and reward yourself for keeping to them, measuring your feelings before, during and after exposure to the objects of your desire is a good way to move forward.

I have worked with children addicted to sugar and sweets who have been 'allowed' to fill up a pillowcase with sweets and then gorge. They have done this for a day, and then got fed up (literally). By giving them permission you can allow them to find their own level (obviously making them have a mega-toothbrushing session afterwards).

Many people find they need to cut out an addictive behaviour altogether to tackle their addiction, whether that addiction is trawling the Internet for porn or smoking cigarettes or drinking alcohol. However, cutting something out does not necessarily mean they will get rid of the obsessional thoughts and feelings that accompany their addiction. That usually takes more time and effort to achieve, using Thought Records and exposure techniques.

### Insight

A note on exposure techniques

CBT is well known for introducing people to the very thing they are scared of in 'gradual exposure' experiments. If you are scared of flying, you might go and sit in a flight simulator. If you hate snakes, you might just go to a pet shop and look at one through safety glass. If you need to be clean all the time, you might 'risk' eating something that dropped on the floor. I once counselled someone who was terrified of their driving test, and we spent two sessions just sitting in the car, with him holding the steering wheel, and wriggling the gear stick, while he sweated and shook profusely. Just sitting in a car was enough for starters. I'm pleased to say he passed his test a few days later, having failed three times before without this kind of preparatory session.

A CBT therapist would help you increase your type and level of exposure until you are able to deal with a full-on situation. For instance, if you are frightened of going out, you may imagine just opening the front door, for starters. Next time, you might actually open it, and the time after that, walk slowly down the front path to the gate. After that success, you might extend your trip to the first lamp post on the street and back, and so on. Each time you would estimate your fear levels before and after, so that you can 'learn' how you are able to manage the experience of the very thing you are frightened of. This kind of gradual exposure experiment is the linchpin of the CBT approach.

Take a moment to think about things you might 'expose' yourself to: stroking a dog, going out in a storm, or speaking in public. Could you imagine doing this the first time? How would it feel?

Try setting up an experiment for yourself. Rate yourself before and after exposure, using the chart on p. 129.

### Change checker

**Maintenance and Safety Behaviours**

Looking back at any of the anxieties and phobias, traumas and obsessions you uncovered earlier in this chapter, are you aware of any maintenance or Safety Behaviours you are adopting, which keep your fears going? Make a note of them.

Can you think of practical ways to expose yourself to things or experiences that will help you reduce your fear? Can you break these down into small, incremental steps? If so, what are they? Again, make a note of these.

Are you aware of any particular 'thinking errors' that help you to keep your anxieties going? Write these down too.

## Exercise and anxiety

Finally, it is well established by researchers that a brilliant antidote to fear and anxiety, and all the associated anxiety disorders, is regular exercise. Most CBT plans for dealing with high levels of anxiety suggest that a daily or weekly exercise regime is an essential way of bringing down fear levels. This is primarily because exercise, particular aerobic exercise, such as swimming or running, stimulates the endorphins in the bloodstream that act as a natural calming agent.

Plan regular exercise into your daily and weekly schedule. Do at least three sessions of 30 minutes of vigorous exercise a week to gain the most rewards. You should, of course, check with a GP before you embark on any new exercise to make sure you are in good enough shape to do it.

However, the more anxious you are the more you will reap the benefits of thrashing up and down a pool, or dancing, or gardening, or playing a team sport, hard and fast. The only caveat will be that, if you are either obsessional or addictive, you don't become addicted to exercise as a means of keeping your weight down. As with everything, you need to remain aware of what you are really doing.

This chapter has covered a huge amount of ground, and I suggest you go back and look at the particular areas that relate to you. Take heart that anxiety is something which can be brought under control with CBT, if you make an effort to be aware of your NATs and physical symptoms the minute they start to surface.

## Your CBT change toolkit

Tool no. 1: Make and stick with your decision to change.

Tool no. 2: Understand how you interpret the world and how you 'tick'.

Tool no. 3: Notice and note down negative thoughts.

Tool no. 4: Track down and eliminate your thinking errors.

Tool no. 5: Clarify problems and conduct experiments.

Tool no. 6: Review your decision, and keep deciding to change.

**Tool no. 7: Conquer your anxiety, phobias, trauma, obsessions and addictions.**

## Homework

If you suffer from anxiety, a phobia, trauma, obsessions or addictions, test yourself by choosing one thing and 'exposing' yourself to dealing with it. Try this once or twice during the next week. Make notes in your Thought Record, focusing in particular on your fear levels before, during and after exposure.

Chapter

8

'One cannot get through life without pain ...
what we can do is choose how to use the
pain life presents to us.'

**Bernie S. Siegel**

# Beating depression: chasing away your 'little black rain cloud'

Depression is no laughing matter. Unfortunately, Eeyore's 'little black rain cloud', which we met in Chapter 3, hangs over many people today, often with distressing and debilitating results. Of course we all have 'down days' and times of 'low mood', when we feel sad or miserable without knowing exactly why. We say we're 'fed up' when we have too much to do, or that we're 'cheesed off' or lethargic when we're bored. Dealing with the ups and downs of our moods is clearly something we all have to manage on a daily basis.

## Stigma

Until fairly recently there has been quite a social stigma about people mentioning the 'D' word in public. Probably before the arrival and untimely demise of Princess, then Lady Diana, 'depression' was a dirty word. Now, in our celebrity-obsessed culture, it has become 'normal' for people to talk about their battles with depression. As celebrities such as Robbie Williams, Victoria Beckham or Monty Don have 'owned up' to suffering from depression, it can seem amazing to the rest of us – they seem to have so much going for them. Surely, if people such as Stephen Fry, a national treasure and seeming bon viveur, can talk openly about being depressed, then so can we?

Although there has always been some slack about women being 'emotional' and 'depressed', men have usually had to bury their feelings deep. However, that has also changed as celebrity males have begun to speak more openly about their feelings, or have even cried in public. Gradually the social stigma around depression and mental health has begun to erode, although there is still some way to go.

However, there is a quite a big difference between feeling a bit glum or down in the dumps and actually becoming depressed. So this chapter is going to look at the issue of depression in more detail and, in particular, what CBT can do to help you conquer it for yourself.

Basically, if you feel depressed, you will probably feel:

- a lack of pleasure in things or a loss of enjoyment
- everything feels difficult to do, no matter how small or easy
- overwhelmed with a sense of dread at all there is to do
- lethargy at the thought of doing anything at all
- no interest in seeing or talking to others
- broody and ruminative, chewing things over and over.

**❝**When the heart weeps for what it has lost, the spirit laughs for what it has found.**❞**                                                                    **Sufi aphorism**

## Specific triggers

Depression can be triggered by many things: women may have cyclical moodiness, and may well feel 'blue' around their 'time of the month'. A new mother might also feel 'down' after the birth of a baby (which is supposed to be a joyful occasion), and a middle-aged woman might feel moody and forlorn with the onset of the menopause.

Men can also suffer from the hormonally-induced downer of mid-life, when testosterone levels drop, midriff weight increases and hair recedes, even if they are not strictly 'menopausal'. Men can also become very low and depressed when faced with life's challenges, such as separation and divorce, redundancy and retirement or loss of sexual prowess. In fact, men often fare worse as they have fewer 'support' systems of friends and family than women, so they need to make an extra effort to battle against the 'black dog' days.

Ironically one of the major conundrums of modern life is that, although our material world has never been so plentiful (in the West, at least), we've never been so dissatisfied or depressed. Sadly, it's estimated by the UK mental health charity, MIND, that around 1 in 10 adults in the UK will experience some level of depression at any one time. Plus, 1 in 20 suffer from the most severe or major type of mental distress, known as 'clinical depression'. Although these statistics seem alarming, at least it means you are not alone if you are feeling low, or suffer regularly from depression.

The good news is that CBT has an excellent proven track record for dealing with depression and related issues. So take heart that something can be done about a condition that can seem so hard to tackle at the outset. Indeed, learning to ride the roller-coaster of our emotions is all part of life. When people become seriously depressed – and depression hangs around for longer than a week or two – it's time to take action.

## The relationship between anxiety and depression

In the previous chapter we saw that anxiety (and all the other issues connected with fear), can lead to feelings of depression. It's equally true that feelings of depression, even short-lived ones, can lead to increased anxiety. So there is often a *symbiotic* relationship between anxiety and depression, with each keeping the other one going, like good old best friends.

## Symptoms of depression

Everyone is different and depression may take many different forms, because it has different triggers. You might just be experiencing 'low moods' or feeling fed up, or there might be something more serious going on. If you become depressed for any reason, there are some fairly universal signs that you might be suffering without you fully realising it yourself.

Take a moment to think about the following symptoms – do they reflect what you have been going through or are currently experiencing? Or have you ever felt any of these symptoms in the past? Jot down your answers.

---

### Test yourself

**Depression symptoms**

- waking up early, sleeping more or finding it hard to drop off to sleep, or get to sleep at all;
- waking up in the early hours and not being able to get back to sleep;
- not eating properly or putting on weight;
- crying a lot, for no apparent reason;
- feeling tired, lethargic, doing less and less, 'shutting down';
- wanting to numb out feelings with substances such as alcohol, tobacco, legal and illegal drugs, pornography, computer use, TV – and using them/doing it more than usual;
- feeling restless and agitated, finding it hard to concentrate;
- finding it hard to remember things;
- having physical aches and pains, heavy legs, headaches – without any apparent reason;
- feeling numb, heavy, despairing;
- lack of sexual interest (low libido);
- finding it hard to make decisions;
- feeling helpless, and preoccupied with negative thoughts (thinking errors);
- lack of self-confidence, self-esteem or positive perspective;
- distancing yourself from others, finding it hard to ask for help;

---

- feeling there's no future, it's all bleak ahead;
- having urges to self-harm or actually doing it;
- blaming yourself, feeling guilty/blaming others, feeling envy;
- feeling unusually intolerant, irritable, bad tempered most of the time;
- not getting pleasure out of things you used to find pleasurable;
- feeling unreal, detached, in a 'bubble';
- feeling suicidal.

(Adapted from MIND's *Understanding Depression* booklet.)

## Change checker

**Do you need help?**

How many of these symptoms do you recognise in your own life? If it's more than, say, four or five, you must get some help *right now* – even if it's just talking to a partner or friend about how you feel. If it's five upwards, and it's been happening for some time (more than two or three weeks), you should go to your GP immediately. You could even ask to be referred to an NHS-funded CBT therapist.

However, if you feel you have many of these symptoms and they've been building up for a long time, then it is essential you get help as soon as possible, as depression needs to be nipped in the bud before it settles into a long-term condition. It's harder to shift (though not impossible) if it's been left to become entrenched over a long time.

## Don't panic

Obviously this is a long list of symptoms, and you may be feeling, or have felt, some, or most of these at one time. You might feel panicked just reading this list, or feel scared of acknowledging that you are depressed because of what it might mean, but there is no need to feel either worried or even ashamed about admitting to having these feelings. They're just feelings, after all.

Remember, you're a human being, and all of these feelings are part of the human condition. It is also true that if you are feeling lethargic and hopeless the last thing you'll probably feel like doing is actually the very thing you need to do. Of course, it can be very difficult to help yourself when you feel helpless, but in fact it's exactly what you need to do if you want to conquer your 'black dog' days.

## Typical depressed negative thoughts

If you get depressed your thinking will begin to run along fairly narrow, darkening lines. It is as if the 'little black rain cloud' has come to your house and is hovering overhead, waiting to follow you wherever you go. The typical negative thoughts that go with your mood might be as shown:

**About yourself:**

- 'I'm a waste of space, I'm totally useless.'
- 'I'm ugly and totally unlovable.'
- 'Nothing ever goes right for me.'
- 'My life is over.'
- 'I'm different: I just don't fit in.'

**About other people:**

- 'Everyone's out for themselves.'
- 'Nobody really cares about me.'
- 'I'm hated and despised by everyone.'

**About life in general/the future:**

- 'What's the point, we're all going to die, anyway?'
- 'Future? What future?'
- 'The world's a dangerous place – full of nasty people grabbing it all for themselves.'

### Depressive 'thinking errors'

These kinds of negative thoughts lead, inevitably, to the kinds of extreme 'thinking errors' we met in Chapter 4. Typically, the main ones are 'catastrophising', 'black and white' thinking, 'filtering', 'personalising' and 'generalising'. The problem is that once a depressive perspective has taken over, then all the black thoughts seem to fall into line, meaning they create even more depressive thoughts and become an ever-increasing downward spiral.

## Activity scheduling

People get depressed for all sorts of reasons. Boiled down, the feelings often amount to **core beliefs** such as:

- **worthlessness**    ('I don't deserve anything');
- **hopelessness**    ('What's the point?');
- **lethargy**    ('I can't be bothered');
- **pessimism**    ('I'm lazy, inadequate');
- **self-blame**    ('It's all my fault');
- **self-criticism**    ('I'm useless')

One of the tried and tested methods in CBT is to try to help people get unstuck. Even the smallest possible start is a good thing. You are encouraged to set out your week, hour by hour, and write down at the end of each hour, precisely what you have done. Even if it just amounts to writing down ordinary things such as making a cup of tea, feeding the birds, putting the bin bag in the wheelie bin, walking to the corner shop, washing your hair. Because each of these activities can seem like climbing Everest when you're down, it's important to pat yourself on the back each time you do anything at all. So noting them down is the first step towards conquering your black moods.

---

Melanie, 35, a single woman working in a retail chain, felt she was doing 'nothing' with her life. She had recently lost her job when her company went into liquidation, and she was finding it hard to get a new one. As time went by, Melanie lay in bed most of the day, watching TV. At night she would drive around in her car, aimlessly, not wanting to see people. Eventually she saw the doctor for a persistent cold, who sussed she was depressed. He suggested she try to do one thing every day to move herself forward.

After some initial reluctance, Melanie began to keep a timetable of her 'activities' and it started to move her off the bottom of the spiral. She even noted down every day commonplace things such as 'had a bath' or 'watered the plants' after she had done them. At the end of the day she could read her list and she began to see that she was not actually 'doing nothing', as she had previously thought. After a month of keeping daily records Melanie found herself strong enough to begin applying for jobs.

---

You'll soon see, for yourself, as Melanie above did, that you don't do 'nothing' with your day. In fact, your day is probably stacked with all sorts of activities, which you dismissed before as not important. Also, you can start planning in pleasures, things that you like to do, that you might think you haven't got time for or don't deserve.

Your weekly activity schedule

(P = pleasure, A = achievement)

| Time of day | Monday | Tuesday | Wednesday | Thursday | Friday | Saturday | Sunday |
|---|---|---|---|---|---|---|---|
| 6–7 | | | | | | | |
| 7–8 | get up, get breakfast, feed cat (A) | | | | | | |
| 8–9 | get kids to school (A) | | | | | | |
| 9–10 | go to work (A) | | | | | | |
| 10–11 | | | | | | | |

| Time of day | Monday | Tuesday | Wednesday | Thursday | Friday | Saturday | Sunday |
|---|---|---|---|---|---|---|---|
| 11–12 | see dentist (A) | | | | | | |
| 12–1 | lunch (A/P) | | | | | | |
| 1–2 | | | | | | | |
| 2–3 | pick up kids (A) | | | | | | |
| 3–4 | hang out wash (A) | | | | | | |
| 4–5 | cook tea (A) | | | | | | |
| 5–6 | | | | | | | |

| Time of day | Monday | Tuesday | Wednesday | Thursday | Friday | Saturday | Sunday |
|---|---|---|---|---|---|---|---|
| 6–7 | kids to bed (A) | | | | | | |
| 7–9 | cinema with friend (P) | | | | | | |
| 9–10 | pub drink (P) | | | | | | |
| 10–11 | bed | | | | | | |
| 11–12 | | | | | | | |
| 12–1 | | | | | | | |

### Your daily log

To get a handle on your depression, you are encouraged to fill in the schedule, at the end of each hour, with descriptions of what you did in the time. You should mark entries with a P for Pleasure or A for Achievement. 'P' might be for things like having a cup of tea, going for a stroll or cleaning out a drawer. 'A' would be for something that you find hard to do, such as making a phone call or cleaning the kitchen surfaces. Keep doing this and, eventually, you will notice a benefit from seeing both how you use your time and that you are, in fact, achieving things and having some pleasure.

# Understanding your depression

You can go through life not really understanding where your depression has come from, so this section is just to give you some pointers as to where it might have originated. Of course, your situation is unique to you, so you will obviously have your own specific reasons for, or particular incidents prompting, getting depressed. For some people the roots will lie in their childhood.

### Role of childhood experiences: *'a predisposition to depression'*

There is no doubt that having a tough childhood will probably make it harder (but by no means impossible) for people to be relaxed and happy in adulthood. Even though CBT is not particularly interested in *analysing* the past, in a psychotherapeutic manner (it is focused very much on improving life in the 'here and now'), there is nonetheless a tacit understanding that the further back our troubles and difficulties go, the more they will probably be feeding into our negative thinking patterns.

Indeed, Aaron T. Beck, the founder of CBT, believed a major precursor for depression in adults was the unleashing of buried feelings from bad childhood experiences by particular triggers in adult life. For example, if your marriage breaks down it can remind you of an irreversible loss, such as losing a parent when you were a child.

Beck believed that a major life event, such as divorce, would not be sufficient in itself to trigger depression unless a person was sensitive or vulnerable for some reason. This explains, to some extent, the age-old conundrum of why two people can experience the same kind of event, and yet come out of it so completely differently:

- **Fred** is divorced by his wife, who has found someone new, and he begins to drink, slide into bitter depression and hide himself away (his mother died when he was small and he still feels deeply abandoned). He vows never to love again.

- **George** is divorced by his wife, who has found someone new, and he says '*Obviously I'm sad but, it's time to move on*' (he still has a good relationship with his mother and his ex-wife), and he joins a sky-diving club and meets new people. He hopes to have another relationship in time.

In terms of dealing with divorce, two very different people reacting in two very different ways. However Fred, with his early, unresolved loss, is sinking into depressive despair, as the old wound is reopened; while George is able to mourn, but nonetheless moves on.

---

### Test yourself

Your life

Are there any past, childhood issues that you find make you sensitive or vulnerable to incidents in your current life?

---

## Beck's model of depression

This is the way Beck looks at depression:

1. You have an early experience, which sets up irrational dysfunctional assumptions and core beliefs such as '*Nobody loves me*' or '*I'm worthless*'.

2. You experience a 'trigger' incident in adult life, which stirs up the dormant DAs and CBs.

3. These DAs create, in turn, masses of NATs, which flood your mind – so you become unhealthily preoccupied: *'I'm all alone'*, *'My life's worth nothing'*, *'No one cares about me'*, *'I don't want to see anyone'*; *'I'm unlovable'*.

4. You experience:

   a) distorted thought processes

   b) emotional and physical symptoms of depression.

Beck's model is illustrated in the diagram below.

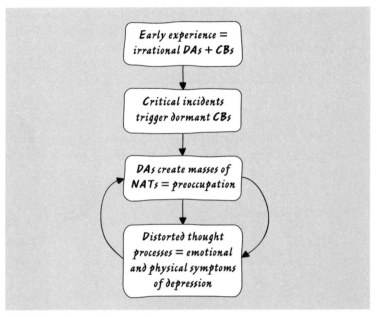

*Beck's model of depression*

## The main types of depression

Depression is a generic term, but it tends to break down into the following types of experience.

## Reactive depression

Many episodes of depression can be triggered by past unre-solved issues (as we have seen above), from childhood abuse, sexual violence, or trauma in adulthood, such as rape or an assault. War veterans, accident survivors, people caught up in disasters and car crashes can suffer from **reactive depression**. This needs treating as soon as possible, so that it does not become clinical and long term.

- Ben had worked as a broker for 30 years in the City until he was told callously one lunchtime that he had been 'let go'. He was frogmarched out of the building, and he hit the pub. He was so ashamed, he didn't tell his family he'd lost his job for a month. Instead he went out each day and drank, and then rolled home, pretending he'd been to work. Once he owned up he slipped into a deep depression and spent months in bed. Only when the house was repossessed did Ben finally rally – especially when his wife said she'd leave if he didn't go to the GP.

## Postnatal depression

Many mums of newborn babies suffer from postnatal depres-sion, and it usually kicks in after a couple of weeks, typically usually associated with the drop and change in hormones after birth. However, in some cases it can continue for up to two years, or even beyond, especially if undiagnosed and untreated.

## Bipolar disorder (manic depression)

This kind of disorder is well known for its mood swings. The sufferer is 'high' in a manic phase and then crashes into a 'low' depressed stage. People often find themselves 'functioning' highly and then 'flopping' into a low-energy exhaustion. Bipolar may be down to biochemical imbalances, and may also be genet-ically passed on.

### Seasonal affective disorder (SAD)

Only just beginning to be acknowledged properly in the UK, sufferers begins to feel low when the light fades in September, and then through winter. They find it hard to exist without natural light (which boosts the serotonin levels in the brain), and may want to stay in bed, under the duvet, and hibernate until spring.

SAD is also connected to how Vitamin D is processed – so 20 minutes of light a day on the back of the brain (hypothalamus) a day can make a big difference. Just popping into the garden or out to the shops can stimulate your brain with light. You can even buy a light-box for your office to help boost invaluable serotonin and vitamin levels.

### Clinical depression

This is the term for depression that has continued for a long time and become entrenched. It is 'clinical' because there is a checklist of symptoms that a GP and a psychiatrist use to establish the level and kind of depression you are suffering from.

## Dealing with suicidal thoughts

From time to time, when things get very tough, depression can lead on to bleak feelings of suicide. This can take the form of sudden flashes of desire to 'end it all', or a feeling of hitting a black wall and not knowing if there is a way back. Also, as we saw in Chapter 7, you might start having 'obsessive' thoughts and compulsions to hurt yourself in some way, such as self-mutilation or throwing yourself off something, which also includes wanting to destroy yourself.

If you feel or have felt suicidal **it is important to know and remember:**

● This mood, this moment, this feeling, will pass – *it always does, no matter how intense or despairing it feels at the time.*

- Thousands, if not millions of people in the world feel similarly every day. This does not take your pain away, but you are not alone in feeling engulfed by the blackness from time to time.

- Sometimes you feel suicidal because you are sleep deprived, or recovering from an illness, or have had a shock and can't see past the current situation (such as a partner leaving you, losing a job, losing money, getting cancer). You need to get some sleep, some nourishing food, to follow the steps in this chapter, and get some exercise or relax. You will begin to gain a perspective over time as to how you can move on.

- Break the power of the moment – when you feel suicidal – by telling someone. Call the Samaritans (they're there 24/7 on 08457 90 90 90).

- If you are on the verge, call your doctor, 999, go to A & E, tell a friend, do *something* to curb your desire to hurt yourself.

- Join a support group or find a therapist (www.babcp.co.uk; www.bps.co.uk).

# Understanding and dealing with your depression

A keynote of depression is feeling overwhelmed, helpless, overloaded, unable to cope. We've all been there at some time. It is important to break things down into small chunks, tiny manageable steps, so you can start to move forward.

## Identifying your difficulties

If you are feeling depressed at the moment, or you know you are vulnerable to depression, then you need to focus on what is the main source of your gloom and doom. Try to be aware of what triggers your episodes. Work out the top three most common triggers for yourself from the list below. Is it:

- Your relationship?
- Your work or business?
- Being unemployed?

- Your sex life?
- Your children (if you have any or lack of them)?
- Your physical health or state?
- Your money situation?
- Your housing?
- Your wider environment?
- Your education and prospects?
- Your wider family?
- Your future?

Also, if you have recurrent episodes of depression, answer the following:

- Have you been here before?
- If so, what did you do about it?
- Have you met anyone else with this problem?
- Have you ever confided in anyone about it? Could you do so again?
- If you were your own best friend, or mum, how would you suggest you go about dealing with it?

Notice your answers. Can you now decide, in the 'here and now' to go with one of your solutions? Particularly if it moves you forward, out of isolation. So you talk to someone, reach out for help, do something practical to get yourself going. This is nearly always effective.

## Problem solve

Because depressive feelings are often feelings of helplessness and hopelessness, it's important to solve the problems that can seem utterly overwhelming. Try and be constructive and find at least three things you can do to solve a particular problem – it might be about money, childcare, moving house, finding a job. Whatever it is, once you can break a task into small bits, and tackle one part at a time, you will start to feel better because you'll feel more in control.

You are a worthwhile person, worthy of being alive, even if:

- you have no money, inheritance, savings
- you haven't had children
- you don't own a car
- you're not classically 'beautiful'
- you're disabled
- you're not famous or clever.

All these are constructs that are put on people to make them feel 'less than', and when you are down it's easy to latch on to them and give yourself a hard time.

Focus on the things you *can* do, the person you are. Make a list of your positive qualities, the things you have achieved, the people who like you. Put these lists on your fridge and in your diary.

**❝**The real voyage of discovery consists not in seeking new landscapes but in having new eyes.**❞**      **Marcel Proust**

## Maintaining your depression

As we have seen in previous chapters, CBT believes that we can keep our negative emotional states going by adopting unhelpful 'Safety Behaviours'. Depression is no different – so if you are feeling down, you will probably hide yourself away or have less contact with friends, which, in turn, will increase your feeling of isolation and depression.

This is called a **maintenance process** by Beck, and it is one of the things you have to learn to break out of when you want to change your depression into something more life affirming.

As with most of the ideas in CBT, a maintenance process literally maintains your bad mood by making you go around in a circle. You feel bad, you have negative thoughts, you isolate yourself, you feel you can't cope, you get stuck, and this, in turn, increases your negative feelings of hopelessness, helplessness, self-loathing, and so on. It becomes a vicious circle. Round and round you go. Going nowhere. See the diagram below for a typical maintenance process.

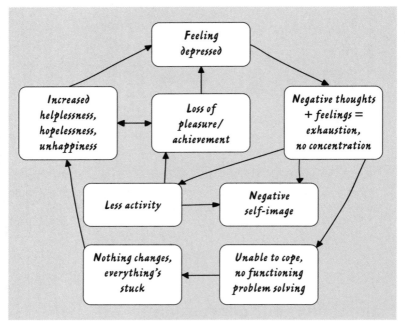

*Typical maintenance processes in depression*

## Mood changers

If you want to break the cycle of depression, and change your feelings, your behaviour and your thoughts, then you have to do something to stop the depressive maintenance process. One thing to do, from the outset, is to have a go at changing your mood.

**What do you find changes your mood? Mood can be changed by**:

1. **deciding to do something differently** (smile, hug someone, play music, listen to a favourite track (A for Activity), put on a bright colour);

2. **changing your situation** (go out for a walk, phone a friend, do some gardening, go for a swim);

3. **reminding yourself of what is going well** – no matter how trivial;

4. **giving yourself a treat, no matter how small** (P for Pleasure);

5. **getting enough sleep** – it's amazing how much sleep deprivation will affect our mood swings.

**Keep and read your records.**

Using your CBT Thought Record and/or Activity Record, you need to note down how you feel before you do your activity, and any negative thoughts. So if you decide to sit in the garden in the sun and have a drink, you might feel (90 per cent sure) that it will *'make no difference'* before you do it. Afterwards, note down how you feel – it might now be (70 per cent OK), and *'actually feel a bit better'*.

With depression, it is all about incremental steps towards finding a solution that is right for you. You then can become more powerful over feelings that threaten to take you over.

Don't forget to remember, all the time, the link between: **your feelings, thoughts and behaviours**.

## Tips for taking steps – review

- Keep the solution small, but give yourself a time limit to do it in.
- Do it.
- Monitor how you felt doing it.
- Congratulate yourself for doing it.
- Try and remember that you did it, even though you were feeling bad at the time.
- Make a note in your diary, in your notebook or on your computer that you did it successfully (even if it was just phoning a friend), so you can remind yourself next time what you did, and that it was successful.

## Keep yourself active

1. Give yourself an Activity Schedule for your week, especially if you have recently lost your job, are self-employed, recently out of hospital, or newly bereaved.

2. You need to break down your days into hourly slots, and then give yourself targets. Include some exercise, some relaxation, some meditation, some fresh air, at some time in each day.

3. Stick to it, whether you feel like it or not. Avoid staying in bed, going to sleep, blanking out in front of the TV, sitting in the bath for hours – all of which will not move you forward if this is how you escape. It will increase your depression to do this.

4. Also, try not to 'drown your sorrows' in alcohol or other addictive substances, as they will drown you. Alcohol is a depressant, as are many other mood-altering substances.

## Therapy or drugs?

When people get depressed there is an assumption that they should go to their GP and 'get something' to help. The use of antidepressants has been the subject of much debate and controversy over the years, since the Rolling Stones wrote *Mother's Little Helper* – about women at home using tranquillisers, particularly Valium, to cope with modern-day stress, depression and alienation.

Many people fear being 'labelled' depressive and being pumped full of drugs in a *One Flew Over The Cuckoo's Nest* kind of way (the ground-breaking book by Ken Kesey which was made famous by the brilliant film released in 1975 starring Jack Nicholson). The fear of taking being forced to take antidepressant drugs keeps many people (especially men), away from going to a doctor. There's the fear of a stigma being attached to them, especially of having an NHS file and for being labelled 'mentally ill'.

However, according to NICE (The National Institute of Health and Clinical Excellence) the limited and careful use of antidepressant medication can be extremely helpful, especially with the new generation of depression medication that has come in over the past 20 years or so. Thus, the combination of modern medication and CBT therapy can actually be the best way to combat depression for some people. The drugs can take the edge off any debilitating symptoms, while the therapy begins to take hold and get you moving.

**Remember: CBT can start working straight away, and people can see significant changes after about six weeks, even with something as challenging as depression to shift.**

Sometimes the carefully monitored use of antidepressants alongside CBT can provide enough respite, especially when the depression has been triggered by a trauma, such as an accident, shock or bereavement; or is to do with a specific, identifiable event or situation (such as a divorce or an assault), where you need to keep functioning for the sake of the children, or to earn money.

However, any decisions about medication must be discussed with your GP and/or therapist, and you should never self-medicate, or come off drugs suddenly, without seeking professional, medical advice.

## Alternative remedies

If you feel strongly that you don't want to take medication you may want to experiment with alternative means of coping with periods of depression. The use of St John's wort, acupuncture, aromatherapy, homoeopathy and Bach Flower Remedies, and other alternative treatments, have all been used by people experiencing low mood and depression.

These treatments mobilise the body's natural resources to heal itself, such as the production of endorphins (the 'feel-good' hormones), and the stimulation of serotonin and other important biochemicals. They can usually be used safely alongside CBT therapy.

*However, it is* essential *to check with a pharmacist or your GP before taking alternative remedies as they may interfere with other medication you might be taking.*

**❝**One is happy as a result of one's own efforts, once one knows the necessary ingredients of happiness – simple tastes, a certain degree of courage, self-denial to a point, love of work, and above all, a clear conscience. Happiness is no vague dream, of that I now feel certain.**❞**

George Sand

## Onwards and upwards

If you decide to conquer your depression, make sure you give yourself an easy time of it:

- Set realistic goals.
- Be kind to yourself.
- Start small.
- Exercise daily, even the tiniest walk.
- Keep your Thought Records.
- Take it one step at a time.

Plus, if you relapse, just remind yourself that to err is human, and so you can start again, the very next second, the very next day, to chase away your 'little black rain cloud'.

---

### Your CBT change toolkit

Tool no. 1: Make and stick with your decision to change.

Tool no. 2: Understand how you interpret the world and how you 'tick'.

Tool no. 3: Notice and note down negative thoughts.

Tool no. 4: Track down and eliminate your thinking errors.

Tool no. 5: Clarify problems and conduct experiments.

Tool no. 6: Review your decision, and keep deciding to change.

Tool no. 7: Conquer your anxiety, phobias, trauma, obsessions and addictions.

**Tool no 8: Chase away your 'little black rain cloud'.**

---

**Homework**

If you suffer from low mood or depression, keep your activity chart for the next week (see p. 185).
Really work hard at keeping to your timetable. Note down in your Thought Record any shifts in feeling, or rise in mood.
Give yourself a treat for filling in your notes and following your chart.

And finally, one of the major emotions that underpins depression is *anger,* and it is to this – the flame-breathing dragon – that we now turn.

**Chapter**

**9**

'The only devils in the world are those running in our own hearts. That is where the battle should be fought.'

**Mahatma Gandhi**

# Slaying the dragon: channelling your anger

I live on a street in London which is a bit of a 'rat run', with cars always squeezing past each other daily. The red-faced drivers shout abuse at the other drivers out of their windows with unbridled fury and frustration. The road rage incidents can get so out of hand and sometimes escalate, not only into ugly rows, but also into full-on fisticuffs. I've seen running battles ensue down the street, in broad daylight.

It seems to me (from the safe viewing point in my office overlooking the street, of course,) that people almost use the 'excuse' of having someone to scream obscenities at to release all their pent-up frustrations about the rest of their lives. These may include the incessant irritations and frustrations beyond their control; the work pressures, money worries, relationship problems, family demands, health issues and so much more.

## The purpose of anger

Of course anger, like fear, has a purpose. It's a major emotion, an enormous force in life, that is largely to do with our need and desire to survive as human beings. Our anger response is 'hard-wired' as part of the 'fight, flight or freeze' response to threat – it's obviously the 'fight' part (especially on my road). However, I always think of anger and fear as being two sides of the same emotional coin. There is an immense amount of fear, anxiety and even grief mixed up in anger, and although it is an emotion that is mainly concerned with survival, it can become a destructive force if not handled properly.

Increasingly we hear reports about anger being out of control in our society. We hear distressing stories about bullying, harassment, muggings, stabbings, wars, and the terrible abuse of children. It makes for daily grim reading in the papers.

The question is: are we angrier now than we used to be, in the bad old days? Or are we letting our feelings out more now, in an unbridled, un-British kind of way? Perhaps a further question to consider here is whether the increase in our addictive behaviours and use of mind-altering substances are contributing to our societal anger surge. Are we are less inhibited, as well as more stressed, befuddled and over-stimulated, and that potent mix is leading to even more 'happy slappy', *Clockwork Orange*-style aggression? Or has the anger always been there and we are just letting rip more?

## CBT and anger

Luckily, CBT has been proven to be extremely effective in dealing with anger. As we have seen in this book, CBT is about learning to notice your **negative thoughts** and track your **thinking errors** in order to be able to change your behaviour. With anger, it is vitally important to be able to locate your **triggers** and **hot thoughts**, as indeed, you can react in an angry way even before your negative thoughts have become in any way conscious. As with anxiety and fear, anger is such an autonomic, intuitive reaction to a stimulus. To interrupt any knee-jerk, destructive behaviour will have to be a deliberate act of aware cognition – in other words, you'll have to think about it to stop it happening.

**"When anger rises, think of the consequences."**     Confucius

The other day I was coming back on the London Underground late at night, having gone to a lovely concert with my daughter and some friends. A very drunken man at the bottom of the escalator started

shouting at us *'Hey, what time of night do you call this?'* I turned around, surprised. I looked at him and I could see instantly that he was squaring up for a fight. *'Yes, you bitch'*, he slurred, *'how dare you keep your kiddies up this late? You're a rotten parent.'* He sounded menacing, and the outraged part of me wanted to shout back, to defend myself. However, I was able to think, for a split second, before he started drunkenly striding up the steps towards me.

Instead of engaging, I simply ferried our party quietly and quickly up the escalator, and thankfully the man lost interest, staggering back down the steps to the platform, mumbling his obscenities to himself. I had felt scared and angered myself at the intrusion, but being able to think for a moment, rather than react, I realised the best course of action was evasive. Otherwise the situation would have quickly escalated out of control, going who-knows-where.

Handling other people's anger:

| Your anger reaction | |
| --- | --- |
| **Trigger** | **Response** |
| Someone shouts abuse at you | You shout back abuse and/or you get into a fight? |

| Your anger reaction with CBT help | | |
| --- | --- | --- |
| **Trigger** | **Cognition** | **Response** |
| Someone shouts abuse at you | You think about it You choose | You could shout back or walk away |

The CBT toolkit will give you choices in terms of your responses. The biggest step here is being able to develop the ability to think between the initial trigger and your actual response. Being able to think about something that you would react to automatically puts you in a position of power. It enables you to work out the best thing to do in a heated situation, for yourself and for others. It stops you being purely knee-jerk in your anger responses.

**Test yourself**

Your anger triggers

Stop and think for a second about what triggers your own anger:

- Do you notice what makes you get annoyed, irritated, or really furious? These may be small things, such as someone leaving the toothpaste lid off, someone slapping their child in the supermarket or dropping litter out of their car, or even bigger things, say government spending cuts.

- Jot down the things that spark your anger, and the varying degrees of anger you feel as a consequence. Try using the following headings.

**My anger triggers:**

**Annoyed/irritated; Really annoyed/Irritated; Cross; Angry; Furious**

# Healthy vs. unhealthy anger

Generally speaking, you can divide anger into healthy and unhealthy types. Roughly, this is based on whether the purpose, type and outcome of the anger is positive or negative in nature.

### Healthy anger = positive anger

- is an anger reaction appropriate to the situation;
- helps create a positive outcome in a difficult or challenging situation – may lead to you being **assertive**;
- enables you to be effective yourself in a difficult situation;
- is able to be expressed, but does not go OTT;
- helps you correct what is wrong;
- does not stop you from being able to reason – is quite flexible;
- does not prevent you from listening to what someone else has to say:
- does not get totally out of control instantly;

- may be able to understand that the reason behind something has nothing to do with what you think it is.

## Unhealthy anger = negative anger

- is a reaction inappropriate to the situation;
- leads to a negative outcome in a difficult or challenging situation;
- makes it difficult to assert yourself in a tough situation – may lead to you being **aggressive**;
- goes from 0–100 in less than a second, and can be OTT;
- stops you correcting what is wrong in a situation;
- hinders you being able to reason – is rigid, demanding, inflexible;
- prevents you from being able to listen to what someone else has to say;
- can get out of control instantly, and takes a long time to burn out;
- may take the form of sulking and/or plotting revenge and can go on for a very long time in a festering kind of way;
- is probably unable to understand or believe that the reason behind something has nothing to do with what you think it is – convinced of your interpretation (rigid).

---

### Reality check

**Bodily symptoms of anger**

Because our bodies react to anger before we can actually think, it's important to try and catch any physiological changes once your fury is triggered. Everyone is different, and you may be more or less aware of your own particular kind of responses. Try to notice how you react, which might include the following symptoms:

- increased heart rate/palpitations;
- 'rushing' sensation in the head as the 'red mist' comes down;

---

- feeling on 'red alert' and tense;
- butterflies in the stomach;
- clenched jaw, gritted teeth;
- clenched fists, tense muscles in neck, arms, legs, knees;
- surge of energy, feeling you want to kick and punch something;
- wanting to stare someone out;
- throbbing head, headache, buzzing in head;
- either heightened stance, or crouching over, ready to attack;
- some kind of unusual smell sensation, like burning;
- a feeling that your head will burst;
- wanting to slam out of a room, or smash something;
- putting your foot down on the accelerator.

**Test yourself**

**What triggers your anger?**

Are any of these recognisable as your symptoms? What happens to you when you feel angry?

**"**I was angry with my friend;
I told my wrath, my wrath did end.
I was angry with my foe:
I told it not, my wrath did grow.**"**

William Blake

# Being assertive vs. being aggressive

A great way of combating anger is to learn the difference between being assertive and being aggressive. The former is far healthier than the latter, and is what you need to aim for.

## Being assertive

- This means learning to defend yourself and to stand your ground.

- It also means asking for what you want, and not just hoping someone will read your mind.

- Work out what you want, or what you want to say, and then be clear.

- Don't blame others for making things difficult; take full responsibility for being assertive to get what you want.

- Wait until the right moment to get someone's attention or to say what you need to – pick your time.

- Use words such as '*I would like it if …*' instead of attacking.

- Don't get into a fight, or be rude or swear – a respectful tone is far more forceful than a rant.

## Being aggressive:

- You shoot your mouth off or lash out with your fists before you can think about it.

- If you want something you start shouting or making your anger felt – raising your voice in a shop, pushing in a queue.

- You drive at other people in your car, and hope they get out the way.

- You cut people off in conversation, or talk over them – you haven't got time for fools.

- If someone critcises you, you criticise them twice as hard back – you're no idiot.

You can probably see a big difference between the two approaches. Being assertive includes practising the following:

- **Learn to handle criticism,** and even accept there may be a grain of truth in what someone says to you – which doesn't mean you have to agree with all of what they say. If someone says to you, '*you always dominate the meetings, you talk too much*', instead of getting on your high horse, and defending yourself, you could say, '*yes, I know I like the sound of my own voice. Are* *you feeling you couldn't get a word in?'* And try and listen to their reply without reacting.

- **Handle your feelings of anger** – and find the right time and way to put someone straight if you feel they've done something to upset you. Don't let your anger fester, as it will grow into something more enormous and aggressive. A friend staying in my house offered to do the washing and I was horrified she shrank a favourite dress of mine, which was a hand wash. I felt like letting rip and shouting, *'How stupid! Don't you read labels?',* but I knew it was actually my fault as I hadn't pointed out it was a hand wash.

  So I let myself cool down and then said, *'I'm really grateful for you doing the washing, but could you read the labels a bit more carefully next time?'*

- **Keep to the point** – a lot of arguments arise and escalate because every past misdemeanour gets thrown into the arena. Try and keep to the point of what you are saying, and leave it at that. If the other person tries to throw everything at you, say calmly, *'Actually, I'd like to talk about x, not y',* and keep to the point. Also, be prepared to walk away.

- **Pick your time** – don't try and work things out if you have been drinking, or it's late and you are tired, or you are driving. It's always better to have a cooling-off period, to go away and think, hack the garden down, have some exercise, do another activity, sleep and in time your anger will have gone off the boil.

- **Prioritise assertion over aggression** – which will mean 'letting go' of some things because they are simply not worth getting into a fight over. You don't have to prove yourself right on every point.

- **Let go of having the last word** – how often in fights do you feel it is necessary that you have 'the last word' so you can prove that you are superior? If you are going round in circles, and the argument is going on and on, and getting nowhere, say, *'I think we'll need to agree to disagree and come back to this later'* or *'Sorry, I really can't do this now, can we please leave it?'*

**"**Rather light a candle than complain about the darkness.**"**

**Chinese proverb**

# Repression vs. explosion

## Different therapeutic approaches

If we took a time machine trip back to the Victorian era, or even the early twentieth century, we would find a great deal of repression in our culture. Many feelings were suppressed, and the expression of anger was one of those behaviours that was considered 'unseemly'. Of course, how much you repressed your anger depended also on your class background, age, race and gender.

It was believed to be 'unbecoming' for women to show their anger, or middle- or upper-class people to show their feelings. In a way, we still carry these notions of needing to repress our angry feelings – so much effort can go into trying to control or repress how we really feel. It's still thought women's anger is somehow 'worse' than men's, and there is more of an outcry when women are angry or violent.

However, there is quite a lot of evidence that repressed anger can lead to health problems concerning our respiratory and cardiovascular systems. Some people think there is also a link between repressed anger and cancer. Certainly, repressing violent feelings can cause stomach and digestive problems, migraine headaches, and affect sleep and general health. Thus the idea of simply repressing angry feelings to deal with them is probably not a healthy, life-affirming one.

## Letting it all hang out (not)

The 1960s hippy era was a 'letting-it-all-hang-out' reaction to the end of Victorian/Edwardian repression and the stringencies of the Second World War era. In the late fifties and sixties, the reaction to repression led many to want to let their hair down (literally), and let rip. Many of the emerging 'new age' movements had their roots in therapies such as Primal Scream Therapy, and encounter groups stemmed from the desire to overturn any type of emotional constipation.

Consequently, there was a lot of shouting and emoting, bashing of pillows and screaming in the getting-it-off-your-chest-peer-type therapies, which were helpful, but today many psychologists believe these therapies did not go far enough to marry cognition to behaviour and physiology in a powerful CBT way. These treatments tend to offer short-term results rather than long-term change.

The issue is what to do with the emotional fallout once it has been released. It's like letting the emotional genie out of the bottle. A good way forward is the CBT mode of operating, which acknowledges the strength of your feelings, notes them, observes them, but does not necessarily focus on them. This is neither repression nor explosion.

**❝Strong in their softness are the sprays of the wisteria creeper; The pine in its hardness is broken by the weak snow.❞**

Master Jukyu

## Understanding the roots of your anger

### Your childhood

For many people, the roots of their anger come from unresolved childhood problems. What your NATs will reveal if you are angry a lot is a constant preoccupation with feeling powerless or overpowered, or what is fair or unfair or discriminatory. You may have experienced specific incidents, such as abuse or attacks, family break-up, sibling rivalry, addiction and chaos, which still affect your adult life.

You may have recurring NATs such as:

- *'I'll get my revenge one day – I'll get even'*;
- *'It's not fair, everyone picks on me'*;

- *'Nobody treats me that way any more – it's disrespectful'*;
- *'The next person who crosses me, gets it'*.

## Negative Core Beliefs

If you've grown up in an unsafe, chaotic household, with dysfunctional parents, you may well end up with extremely negative CBs. Children are necessarily narcissistic, it's what they need to be to survive. However, any adult who has been systematically hurt as a young child, or who has not had their emotional and psychological needs met, may well end up being extremely narcissistic in adulthood. This can lead to a lot of thinking errors, such as extreme personalisation, black and white thinking, and all the others we met earlier. In turn this can lead to a lot of anger.

**"**A clay pot sitting in the sun will always be a clay pot. It has to go through the white heat of the furnace to become porcelain.**"**

Mildred Witte Stouven

# Understanding yourself and your anger better

You don't need to analyse yourself in CBT, but it is useful to understand more about your past distresses so you can handle your anger better.

## Childhood anger triggers

Briefly, people who tend to have issues around anger in adulthood quite often will have experienced one or more of the following.

### Early separation from their mothers or carers

This can be true of people who still feel bereft or resentful in adulthood, especially those who have been in care, fostered, adopted, or there has been a serious interruption in the 'bonding' between mother and child for whatever reason. Family break up through divorce and separation can also add to this relationship being interrupted. In later life issues of **trust** and **worth** and **power**, problems around **love** and **feeling help-less** may arise. Adults can end up being very **narcissistic**, and unable to empathise with others.

- **Darius** was handed around to different foster parents for most of his childhood: now as an adult he feels highly sensitive to any kind of rejection or abandonment. So when his last girlfriend left him, he lashed out and punched her, even though he felt he loved her.

### Violated boundaries

In some unfortunate households the adults breach the boundaries of the children – sexually, emotionally and physically. If one or any of these have occurred, then important psychological boundaries are also crossed, resulting in deep-seated rage. In adulthood, situations that seem similar to the past violations will probably trigger volcanic anger responses. Situations of **betrayal, lack of trust**, and issues around **physical and emotional safety**, will be very explosive:

- **Daisy** absolutely hates it when people come up and start cleaning her car windscreen at traffic lights without asking. It's something that really triggers her fury. She's even put her foot down and driven at the cleaners, so hair-trigger is her anger. With therapy she now understands that her rage goes back to sexual abuse in her childhood, when an uncle used to touch her body forcibly and inappropriately.

### Addiction

Children who grow up in alcoholic homes, or homes with issues around drugs, violence, sex, or a range of other addictive behaviours, may well find it **hard to trust** in adulthood. 'Mind reading' is a typical thinking error, along with 'black and white' polarised thinking, which is prevalent among people who have grown up with addicted parents or carers.

Lack of safety is also an issue, and as it may have been a very scary environment to be in, there is an emphasis on either finding security in adulthood, or living very insecurely. Many people-pleasers come from these backgrounds – but under the people-pleasing behaviour will be a mountain of untapped rage.

- **Jess** always tries hard to please people, and finds he's a bit of a doormat in relationships. He grew up with an alcoholic mother, whom he had to look after. Recently Jess found out that his wife had spent thousands on credit cards, and he hit the roof. She had 'taken advantage' of his generosity, and Jess didn't know how to confront her, so he took his anger out on himself and went and got drunk. He'd grown up seeing his mother 'solve' her problems by drowning them in alcohol, so he did it too.

### Traumas

Some adults have not recovered from the trauma of their childhoods – violent parents, painful splits, having to move country/being refugees, experiencing accidents, fires, and a range of other issues. Trauma particularly leads to an increase in anxiety and fear, but also anger responses (as anger is the flip side of fear). In adulthood, situations can be triggered by flashbacks and experiences that remind people of their past traumas. This can lead to you lashing out or withdrawing and sulking the minute a nerve is touched.

- **Gina** can't cope with anyone getting angry with her, as her father was always shouting and hitting out. She tends to withdraw in an argument and sulk for days. She knows it's destructive, but she'd do anything rather than get into a fight – she's seen enough anger to last her a lifetime.

### Criticism, neglect, abuse

Growing up in a very critical, attacking, judgemental household, where a child is constantly told they are 'not good enough', can create a mountain of repressed anger. Some extremely strict religious households, or families that have a lot of rules, can lead to strong anger responses. If a child feels they have no right to say what they feel or think, or are ignored, neglected, repressed at every turn, this can become a great deal of pent-up rage in adulthood. This can lead to being a resentful, angry adult, who is judgemental and critical themselves – with anger seeping out at every opportunity.

- **Bert** learned to cut off from his feelings from an early age, as he was always under the spotlight of his father's critical gaze. As an adult, Bert is a total perfectionist, and he always picks holes in everything anyone else does. He is never satisfied, always irritable, and as a consequence finds it hard not to pick self-righteous fights with people at home, at work and on the streets.

## The past is over

The good news is: the past is definitely over. There is nothing that you can do to bring it back or change it, even if some terrible childhood experiences can make you want to spend your whole life looking back, over your shoulder, trying to rewrite or analyse the past. Some people even end up in therapy for years and years, desperately trying to heal because the messages in early life were so negative. Of course, if you were brought up to feel you were worthless and unlovable, and you were actively attacked, harmed, traumatised – you may very end up an extremely destructive, angry adult.

I have seen it many times with clients, friends, colleagues and family members, that unchecked anger can be highly poisonous. If anger is turned against yourself or others it can lead to a great deal of self-harm (including addiction) and suicidal thoughts. Some people hold on to their pain, taking revenge, plotting their final vindication. All these thoughts can actually mean they remain stuck in the past rather than being able to live fully in the present.

## The CBT approach to anger

If any of the above rings true for you, then take heart. The CBT approach is to help you identify your NATs and your triggers, and then work out how to combat the angry feelings, thoughts and behaviours as they arise.

## Insight

### Asking for forgiveness

There may well be things that you have done in your life – spurred on by your anger – that you wish you hadn't. You may not be able to repair what you have done, but you may be able to show that you are moving forward, and that you understand why you did it. This can mean a lot to someone if you have hurt them by taking revenge or through lack of trust.

What you can do:

- Write a letter (which you either send or don't), to the person you have hurt, explaining why you did what you did, and saying a genuine 'Sorry'.

- If you can meet someone face to face and say 'Sorry' it is important that you give them time to say how they felt about you hurting them. Try not to defend yourself; try to listen.

- Put into practice new ways of doing things that show people you are moving on. If you have blanked people because you are angry with them, then start making amends. At all times be as genuine as you can be.

- If you have committed any violent crimes, then you may consider what you need to do to repair the mistakes you have made. There are victim support schemes where you can meet your victims face to face, which can have a powerful effect on the rest of your life (let alone theirs).

- Similarly, if you have been unfaithful in a marriage or relationship, you may need to repair the damage by making a genuine apology. This may not make the person you have betrayed feel better, and they may not respond in a way that you want, but it may help you to have tried to repair any damage you have done.

- Also, if you have hurt any children in your care, or children you know, it will be of vital importance to repair as much damage as you can, so as not to continue the cycle of abuse that is handed down from generation to generation.

# Learning to channel your anger

## Slaying the dragon within

If you want to slay your own internal dragon – the fire-breathing being that pops out and blasts everything within reach when you are angry – then you will need to learn some tools.

### Identify your triggers

Go back to p. 215 where we discussed triggers. Make sure you can see clearly what the danger areas are in your life where you tend to 'lose it'.

### Notice your NATs

Continue to keep a Thought Record of your NATs so you can further establish the things that make you rage. If you know you find certain situations difficult, keep track of your NATs so you can be in charge of the situation more and plan ahead, so you are not caught off guard.

### Spot your bodily responses

Because anger can be triggered before you've counted to ten, watch out for the physical changes that mean you're heading for an explosion. Learn to notice the 'warning signs' before the 'red mist' descends. You can do something about it if you know you are in danger of 'going off on one'. Your flight or fight mechanism may be easily triggered, so try and think your way out of situations where you would usually 'blow up'.

### 'Exit, stage right'

Quite often it's a good idea to make an exit rather than stay and fight. If you know you are heading for an angry exchange, you might need to back off before things get too ugly, things get said or thrown, or things get out of hand altogether. Even if you think having a good scrap makes you closer to your partner, or that it asserts your manliness, or strength as a woman, using any form of violence to make your point is always a way to be a loser rather than winner. Learn to exit stage right rather than descend into rage. Count to ten, punch something inanimate. But remove yourself rather than cause damage.

### Blow off steam

A good idea is to take your anger out on a squash ball, a football, the weeds in your garden. Or go for a long run, a long walk, a vigorous swim, a DIY job or a dancing session. Expelling all the pent-up energy in physical activity is a good way of diffusing anger. Even vigorous house cleaning, vacuuming or polishing can be an excellent remedy. Just leave the knife drawer alone, and take yourself away from anything that you could either harm yourself or others with.

### Avoid provocation

If someone is squaring up to you, or shouts at or slaps you at home, try to walk away. Better to avoid the situation, which could get very nasty. If you want to learn some martial arts or physical self-defence tricks to get out of any attacks on the street or at home, make sure that you use the moves that disarm rather than seriously injure or kill your attackers.

### Handle criticism

If being criticised sets your anger off, you are vulnerable 24/7 to your feelings. Learn to detach yourself from whatever is said, and let it go. Swallow your reactions; if you respond in anger things will escalate. Decide to come back to the point at a later time, when you feel less vulnerable.

### Learn to articulate

Violence and aggression often occur when people feel they can't express themselves any other way. Resorting to fists or other violent means seem the only way to 'express' the feeling inside. Use 'I' statements as much as you can, and try not to be provocative. Try to learn to say how you feel so you can assert youself, rather than being aggressive and threatening. Even if you shout it's probably better than resorting to fists.

### Learn controlled anger

Some circumstances (when you are under threat), may need you to exhibit some kind of controlled anger, such as raising your voice or shouting (such as if you are teaching a class of rowdy teenage children, or being accosted on the street).

At these times you have to make sure you shout or assert yourself in such a way as to make an impact, and show you mean business, without actually feeling angry. I call it 'dramatising' anger. If you 'out-dramatise' someone who is shouting at you, or abusing you, they may well quieten down or go away. However, it's a matter of fine judgement as to whether things will escalate. If you sense they will get worse then simply remove yourself from the situation as soon as you can.

### Breathe

If you have been able to learn some relaxation, meditation or mindfulness techniques, try and breathe when you feel anger rising. Because of the autonomic physical responses involved, you will be tensing and tightening your muscles, and beginning to breathe rapidly as your heart beats faster. Try and quell your rage by taking some very deep breaths, counting to three as you do – 1 – 2 – 3 in, 1 – 2 – 3 out, and try to calm yourself down. Closing your eyes for 30 seconds and concentrating on your breathing can also help, as you remove the environmental stimuli that might well be winding you up.

### Disarm your attackers

You may always have been defensive when someone attacks you verbally, or have had to kick back if attacked physically. Learn to be 'cool' by listening and perhaps even agreeing with someone when they have a go at you – this disarms them immediately. If it's a physical attack, learning some disarming moves could come in handy, as long as you don't get involved in a fight.

*Pat yourself on the back*

If you have managed any of the above in a situation where you would usually lose your rag – well done. It can be very difficult to walk away, as you feel you must make your point, or make yourself felt, but if your life has been scattered with anger-fuelled mistakes or incidents you regret, then now is the time to start acting differently. Here and now. Pat yourself on the back every time you manage to get out of a situation and keep things calm. Learning that the past is over, that the current situation may remind you of it, but is not actually it, can be a great step forward on your adult learning curve. Keep aware of your triggers, your NATs, and implement your new strategies, and you should be heading for calmer waters.

**❝**Hatred is the winter of the heart.**❞**                    **Victor Hugo**

# Be strong, not weak

And finally:

- Some people feel that walking away from a fight is weak: it's not. It's very strong.
- Some people also feel that not arguing back is to be trodden on: it's not. It's actually assertive.
- Some people think not answering back is timid: it's not. It's extremely powerful, and full of sound judgement.

## Keep on track

Familiarise yourself with your anger triggers, and keep your Thought Record, teasing out the things you know that make you see red. Learn to make a distinction between assertion and aggression in everyday life and you will be well on your way to slaying the dragon and learning to channel your anger into a positive force for good.

**Your CBT change toolkit**

Tool no. 1: Make and stick with your decision to change.

Tool no. 2: Understand how you interpret the world and how you 'tick'.

Tool no. 3: Notice and note down negative thoughts.

Tool no. 4: Track down and eliminate your thinking errors.

Tool no. 5:  Clarify problems and conduct experiments.

Tool no. 6: Review your decision, and keep deciding to change.

Tool no. 7: Conquer your anxiety, phobias, trauma, obsessions and addictions.

Tool no 8: Chase away your 'little black rain cloud'.

**Tool no 9: Slay the dragon and channel your anger.**

---

**Homework**

Vicious Flower exercise

Make a list of the things that trigger your anger.

Think of a recent or particular event when you lost your temper and fill in the Vicious Flower (see p. 117), being as honest as you can.

**Chapter**

# 10

'The experience of introspection shows ...
that the negative emotions are transitory mental
events that can be obliterated by their opposites,
the positive emotions, acting as antidotes.'

Matthieu Ricard

# Boosting your confidence and self-esteem

An ex-Fleet Street editor once told me this story. He said every year when it was time to negotiate pay rises, the top male journalists would stride into his office, demand 10 per cent, a pension plan, a new top-range car and say they would *'Walk and work for a rival'* if they didn't get it. Meanwhile, the top female journos would either not come into his office and prefer to e-mail him or, if they did come in, sit down, chat for a while and then accept 5 per cent and be grateful. Few would make extra demands, and almost none would ever threaten to *'Walk'*.

What is the difference between these two examples (apart from the obvious, **gender**)? One word: **confidence.** The feeling that you are able to walk in, command attention and a good salary, is a wonderful feeling. This should not be confused with arrogance, or aggression, but rather a feeling of buoyant well-being, born of knowing you are good at what you do, and you deserve to be paid for it. It's about asking, and expecting to be given.

---

### Test yourself

**How confident are you?**

So, how confident are you? Are there situations that would fill you with horror if you had to walk in and be self-assured? Take a second to jot down the places you feel the least and the most confident in your life. It might be being a parent, or at work, or teaching children, or when you are dancing, or performing, or just being alone. Or perhaps you seldom feel that calm, confident buzz?

---

# How to boost your confidence

In fact, it is relatively easy to boost your confidence the CBT way. It is all about recognising the things you already do, and building on them. If you feel unconfident about driving a car, you can sit in the driver's seat and familiarise yourself. Using the typical exposure techniques we have already seen in this book, you can set yourself little experiments, say to drive a short way, noting your thoughts before and afterwards, and writing down how you feel before and after the task.

Confidence-building is just that: each time you do something you will learn that you are more capable, and more able, than you realise. This is because any negative thinking lurking around will be undermining your power to try out something new and build on the experience. So it's time to stop listening to the voice that says '*I can't*' and listen to the one that says '*I can*'.

Eve recently went on an 'outward-bound' course organised through her office for 'team building'. As part of the challenge, she had to abseil down a rock face. Eve hates heights, and was worried about her weight, so point blank refused to do it. However, the instructor and her best work friend spent time getting Eve to talk about her fears. In fact it wasn't so much the height that was the problem, but her self-consciousness about her weight, and she didn't really trust the equipment to hold her. Demonstrating how the ropes and carabiners worked, and offering to abseil alongside her, her two companions eventually boosted Eve's confidence to the point that she was able to have a go. Afterwards, 80 metres later and safely on the ground, flushed and excited, Eve was jubilant. '*Wow! I'm so glad I did it. I feel like I could do anything, now.*'

Of course, learning to boost your own confidence means you may have to face changing your old negative thinking habits, thus giving up on any ideas you have that you are a certain kind of person. This is what change is all about, and is what CBT encourages you to do: boost and build your confidence.

## Remember the 'change paradox'

Indeed, nothing ever stays the same. Life is constantly changing, our circumstances are always presenting us with new challenges and we are always needing to think afresh to meet those challenges. As we saw in Chapter 1, we often say we want to change – *just as long as we don't really have to change*. But everything is changing all the time, in all directions, so change is really about meeting those challenges that are really simply part of living life to the full.

## Self-acceptance

The 'change paradox' also raises issues of self-acceptance. If you are supposed to be changing yourself (in CBT terms this means giving up negative thought patterns and thinking errors), then how can you accept yourself? Some people who are anxious or obsessive, or depressed and angry, feel a lot of the time that they don't like themselves and would like to change absolutely everything about themselves this instant. They can be very 'black and white' and not able to see or accept the parts of themselves that are absolutely fine.

Some people fear that if they accept themselves they will be lazy, arrogant or self-complacent. This is usually just a fear. So the CBT challenge is to accept yourself, to like yourself, and to boost your confidence for yourself – catch yourself when you want to put yourself down, and just don't do it.

**“**Nothing we ever imagine is beyond our powers, only beyond our present self-knowledge.**”**
                                                    **Theodore Roszak**

## Building self-esteem

Also, to build self-esteem, you need to change your core beliefs. If most of these are negative: *('I'm worthless', 'I'm helpless', 'I'm unlovable' or 'I'm evil through and through')*, then you need to set things up in your life so that you build on the good things that you **do**, **feel**, and **think** (Beck's Cognitive Triad, see p. 84).

You need a big, sustainable boost of self-confidence to build your self-esteem. The only way a positive self-image can come about, from the bottom of the glass where your CBs lie, seeping upwards, will be if you start acting and thinking in ways that will ultimately make you feel better about yourself. Remember that CBT is all about the interaction between cognition, behaviour and physiology, and this still continues, as we change and grow.

## How to boost self-esteem, self-confidence and build a positive self-image

1. **This will not happen overnight**. There are no instant remedies or quick fixes. However, there is growing evidence that CBT can also be very effective with issues around addiction, eating disorders, relationships, traumas, depression, anxiety and other problem areas.

2. **Focusing on the positive things** that happen, and building on them, will help you begin to move forward. For instance, if you are 'socially anxious' and assess your fear of going to a party alone at 90 per cent, and then, having gone, reassess your fear level at 70 per cent – this is definitely a step forward. Next time you can remind yourself you felt better about it once you had done it – and you can start the process of going out alone from a different level of fear. This can accumulate until you begin to learn that you can go out alone, and handle the situation, just fine.

3. **Living with imperfection**. A lot of us crave perfection, but none of us are perfect. It's actually an unachievable goal.

Many obsessions and anxieties arise from needing to be perfect, and not accepting that we are human, and therefore fallible. An important part of CBT is focused on learning to live with imperfection, finding the midpoint between the black and white extremes. People with eating disorders and negative self-images are particularly vulnerable to not accepting their imperfection – but you can do this if you use your CBT toolkit to look at the good things that you are able to do and be in your life, despite being imperfect. Any work you can do on accepting that you make mistakes will move you forward.

4. **Catch your 'black bat' NATs** and continue to pin them down, write them down, notice them. If you continue to do this, regularly, methodically, using your Thought Record, you can begin to see how you think, how you create your life, your reality. As you change and grow your NATs may change, too. You need to become an expert NAT-catcher, so you can stop tripping yourself up. When you hear the negative thoughts as you go about your day, you don't need to let them trip you up, or follow their direction. Rather you can think *'Ah, that one again'*, and write it down, or let it go.

5. **Conquering depressive thoughts**. Keep your activity chart for a week, or even just a day, to boost your confidence and self-esteem. Note who calls you, or texts you, and notice what you really do with your time. This will help you feel better about yourself cumulatively.

6. **Slaying your anger**. Every time you resist lashing out, taking revenge, hurting someone, being snappy, or you manage to handle someone else's anger effectively, your self-esteem and self-confidence will be boosted. Notice how effective you are becoming at handling things you might have reacted badly to in the past. If you are avoiding escalating aggression then you are doing brilliantly.

Once she became aware of it, Sara was amazed at how often she put herself down. She said, in therapy, that she found she bullied herself at every possible opportunity. If she missed the bus, she'd think, *'You idiot, you should have left earlier'*, or if she broke the yolk of an egg she was frying, *'Typical, you can't do anything right.'*

Over time, keeping her Thought Record, she realised this critical, negative voice hissing in her ear over and over was reminiscent of her mother who always slapped her with a stream of stinging judgements as a child. *'My mother constantly put me down, told me off and made me feel bad,'* explained Sara. *'She never said "well done", it wasn't in her vocabulary. I would just get a stern look and a pursed lip – whatever I did was never right.'* Sara realised she needed to start appraising herself more accurately.

She realised that most of the eggs she fried didn't break in the pan, so the odd one that did was fine. She was usually very punctual, and actually, when she was late, there were many things that contributed to that happening. Maybe the bus being late wasn't her fault after all. As she stopped slapping herself with bitter internal criticism she began to relax and feel as if like she had to be perfect all the time. Her self-esteem began to grow as she found she actually did things 'right' most of the time. She was able, in time, to turn off the nasty, self-defeating voice that kept tripping her up – and she felt calmer, and happier, as a consequence.

Sara also found she was criticising her own daughter and husband less now that she was easing up on herself. It was a revelation just how much she had sabotaged her own peace of mind and also how much she could do about changing that.

## Insight

Here are some other self-esteem boosting activities, which might also be pleasant and will boost your well-being.

- **Look after your health and diet**. This doesn't mean giving up on enjoyment, but if you eat fresh fruit and vegetables, and watch your fat, salt and sugar intake, you can benefit enormously. Cut back on the junk and you will boost your mood and sense of control in your life. Check out your weight and, if you need to lose some, make sure you do it sensibly and slowly, with a GP's support. Losing about a pound a week is good if you are a bit heavy, but you need to know when to stop. If you join a club to lose weight make sure it is a reputable one, such as Weight Watchers.

- **Cut down on (or cut out) alcohol, nicotine, caffeine, drugs**. If you are trying to blot out difficult feelings with alcohol, drugs or other addictive substances, this will impair your ability to think straight. If you are dealing with the aftermath of a trauma, or relationship break-up, it will be tempting to 'drown your sorrows', but in the end it will lead to more things to have to clean up in your life. A lot of the things we do to 'relax' or 'have fun' or 'chill' are actually harmful, and can create more problems than they solve. You will increase your difficulties in life, especially if you turn to your addictions when you need emotional support. Far better to stick your cravings down in your Thought Record, and start thinking about all the things that you are able to do sober, straight, etc.

- **Groom yourself**. It's easy to let things go if you're feeling down or overburdened. You don't have to have expensive haircuts or clothes, but spending some time making sure you are clean, your hair is trimmed and your nails are cut, will make you feel better about yourself. People tend to neglect their physical appearance when they feel down, so you can invest in some new clothes (even good second-hand ones are a boost) and, for women, a little light make-up (there are plenty of cheap deals around). Just the act of looking after your appearance will make you feel more like 'you're worth it'. Also turn off your critical voice when you look in the mirror – accept who you are – you're fine.

▶

- **Look after your finances**. If you have money difficulties, there is plenty of help around (visit www.citizensadvice. org.uk). You need to help yourself sort out your financial problems because this will boost your confidence in the long term.

- **Take exercise**. So easy to say, so hard to get around to. But once you get the exercise habit you will start to enjoy life more, and feel so much better for it. Your self-esteem will bloom like a spring bouquet. It doesn't have to be costly either – you can go to a local park and walk, go dancing or to a dance class, do some gentle exercise classes to get you going (your local leisure centre should have some). Get moving – there's always exercise and fresh air in pottering around the garden or helping some-one else sort out theirs. Even a little light housework will get you moving – some vacuuming, dusting, or cooking with the radio on or music blasting can actually be fun. Even love-making can count as positive, life-enhancing exercise (as long as you practise safe sex).

## Test yourself

**What do you like about yourself?**

(Don't think '*nothing*'.) It's important to estimate yourself, and like yourself, to boost your self-esteem. Take time to think about yourself and make a list of the things you truly value or just like. Think about your generosity, your kindness, or how you treat animals. Maybe you like your eyes, hair or legs. Whatever, say some nice things to yourself and, if you look in the mirror, try saying, '*I'm fine*' or '*I like me*'. It may seem a silly thing to do at first, but it is important to boost your self-esteem and not put yourself down.

Write down ten things you positively like about yourself as a person.

## Taking responsibility

Another important part of the 'change paradox' concerns examining how responsible you really need to be. Many people who seek help find they are carrying a great deal of responsibility for things in their lives – sometimes way too much. Thus people who are anxious and depressed can tend to think they are responsible for absolutely everything. Feeling overly responsible for everything, all the time, can weigh very heavily on an individual's shoulders. It can lead to deep feelings of guilt, shame and self-loathing.

Carl's 'Responsibility Pie Chart'

| Carl sees the news: | Carl thinks: | Thinking errors |
|---|---|---|
| It says: *'Global warming threatens our health.'* | *'It's all my fault.'* | Personalisation Overgeneralisation Black and white Filtering Blaming Catastrophising |

## Responsibility pies

CBT has a very useful mechanism for helping you work out the appropriate level of responsibility that belongs to you: it's a **responsibility pie.** Instead of blaming yourself and beating yourself up for everything that has happened, a responsibility pie chart helps you work out exactly what belongs to you.

Take the case of Carl, above. He is feeling hugely responsible for global warming affecting health. And, yes, although he probably could do more to recycle or save energy he could draw up a responsibility pie chart as follows.

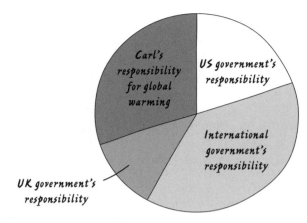

*How Carl views the problem*

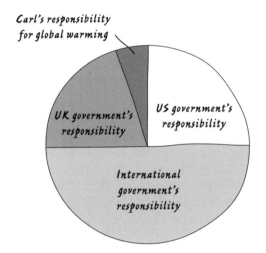

*After CBT approach – review*

**Test yourself**

**Your responsibility pie**

Are there any issues that you feel hugely responsible for, or that overburden you? Do you feel guilty and bad about any things in particular, which you are sure are all your fault? These might be things such as losing a job, your child getting into trouble, an earthquake in Chile, someone getting ill or hurt.

Fill out a chart similar to Carl's, estimating your slice of responsibility.

If you can accurately weigh up your own level of responsibility for things in your life that worry you, or make you obsessed, angry or depressed, you can begin to get a more level perspective. If you do this, you will find you will be able to relax more, feel less responsible (and therefore less anxious) in your everyday life. You will definitely need to teach yourself to be less responsible than you have been, if you have felt 100 per cent responsible for everything.

Some people fear responsibility, and don't want to take on that they are in charge of their own lives and personal growth. If this is true of you, you need to take responsibility for filling in your Thought Record, and sticking to your CBT programme for change.

You will need to keep reminding yourself that it is you who is in the driving seat in your own life, and that it is up to you to keep yourself on track. It's easy to find excuses to slip back into old habits and thinking patterns; but if you want to change, you will have to make the effort to stick at decisions you make about doing things differently in future.

## Goal setting

A central part of the CBT approach to problems involves goal setting. The main way to move forward is to set goals for yourself and stick to them. **SMART goals** are:

**S** – Specific – what exactly, when, where, with whom;
**M** – Measurable – how much, how often;
**A** – Achievable – is it possible for me to achieve?
**R** – Realistic – is it probable?
**T** – Timely – by when?

## Test yourself

**Set up a science experiment on yourself**

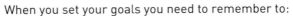

When you set your goals you need to remember to:

- define the problem (and formulate it);
- keep your Thought Record;
- explore which NATs are healthy, or unhealthy;
- notice the thinking errors you tend to have around the problem;
- look at your triggers;
- decide what or how you want to be different in future;
- think how you could behave differently, or think differently, in future, if you experience a trigger;
- estimate how you feel before you go into the situation or experience something;
- decide to deliberately **expose** yourself to a situation where you will be triggered to see if you can act and think differently in the face of the challenge – this is the testing-out part;
- afterwards, register how you felt going into the situation or having the experience – was it as hard as you thought, easier, better? Note these down and keep a record of what you felt, what you thought, and how you reacted physically.

Brian is terrified of public speaking. His boss has made it absolutely clear that he has to give a ten-minute presentation to the sales reps next time they are in town. Brian has explained to his boss that he doesn't want to do it, but his boss is insisting that he has to have a go, particularly as Brian is hoping for promotion, and will thus have to address management meetings in future. Brian is having sleepless nights about the forthcoming speech – he is sweating, shaking, can't eat – as the memory of the time he blanked out at his best friend's wedding when he was best man comes back to haunt him. It was the worst experience of his life, as he had to run from the room, utterly humiliated and embarrassed.

However, Brian really wants the promotion (which is his motivation), and part of him really does want to respond positively to the challenge. So, in preparation, Brian decides to work through his CBT exercise (as outlined in the box above). He knows he would rather avoid speaking (for 'safety reasons'), but that this would 'maintain' his problem (because it wouldn't challenge him to grow). He sets his goal: addressing the meeting. And he prepares his talk. He estimates his fear at 100 per cent – it's that bad.

Brian knows his trigger is his fear of drying up, exactly what happened when he was at the wedding. So this time he makes prompt cards, with the point he wants to make on each card. He also rehearses with his dog, saying the speech to him over and over again. He talks to a friend, who suggests he looks over people's heads, at a point at the back of the room. On the day of the presentation he makes sure he puts on lots of anti-perspirant (he also has a fear of wetting his shirt).

Brian's friend says he can call him on the day for moral support. As he is still terrified, Brian texts his friend just before the meeting. It helps to remind him his friend is there for him. Once in the room, Brian manages to stand in front of the group, although his knees are knocking and his hands are trembling. He is glad he has his cards: he manages to look just over people's heads and even smiles. He starts shakily, but gains confidence and soon is at the end of his prompt cards. He's done it!

At the end of the talk there's a round of applause. In the bar afterwards his boss claps him on the back and says *well done, Brian*. Back home, Brian fills in his chart – he did it, and actually it was only 60 per cent scary this time. That's a drop of 40 per cent! Next time (there'll be a next time?!) it will be easier still, because he'll be starting from 60 per cent and going down.

---

### Insight

**Keeping motivated to change**

It can be tough to motivate yourself to keep moving forward, as we often 'forget' what we have agreed to do with ourselves and our problems. That is one reason why it might be better to see a CBT therapist or join a CBT group dealing with a specific problem or issue. However, if you are keen to try to help yourself, it's not impossible to stay on track. CBT recognises that it can be tough to keep yourself going, so there is an exercise to help you keep in touch with the benefits of change. This is called a **Cost–Benefit Analysis**, a concept that comes originally from economics.

## Cost–Benefit Analysis

With a Cost–Benefit Analysis, you literally weigh up the cost (disadvantage) against the benefit (advantage) in order to work out whether to keep yourself trying out a new behaviour or new way of thinking or feeling.

Back to Brian above, struggling to get the courage to give a talk at work because of his fear of public speaking. If we were to do a Cost–Benefit Analysis for him, it might be something like this:

| Cost (disadvantage) | Benefit (advantage) |
|---|---|
| I may forget what I'm saying and sweat profusely | I can use my prompt cards and a good anti-perspirant |
| I will probably be a terribly nervous speaker and it will show | Although I'll be nervous I'll show my boss I can do it |
| I could get too scared looking at the audience | I can look over their heads |
| It'll scare me to death to do it | I'll be up for promotion if I try |

## Test yourself

**Your own Cost–Benefit Analysis**

Can you take one thing that you know you are avoiding, and think how you might challenge it, in a similar way to Brian?

Write down your challenge.

Now review your costs and benefits. Rate how you feel about the task, say on a scale of 1–100 per cent or 1–10 before you attempt the task.

Then assess your Cost–Benefit Analysis of tackling your task, in the format Brian used.

After you have completed the challenge/task, review the levels on your scale, and also review the costs and benefits again. You may need to write a new set of costs and benefits in the light of your experience.

To keep yourself motivated do this regularly. This way you can keep yourself on the straight and narrow. Give yourself a treat or reward not only for tackling your challenge, but also for filling out your tables and keeping yourself on track. It can take a bit of time to get used to doing it, but after a while you may well find you are beginning to do those things that you have put off or avoided for a very long time. And you're still alive to tell the tale!

> **Insight**
>
> **Relax, exercise and meditate**
>
> As we saw in Chapter 7, it's now well proven by ongoing research that relaxation, exercise and meditation are keys to a long, healthy and happy life. You can learn simple relaxation techniques (see pp. 159–163) and how to exercise regularly (even 10 minutes a day will help increase the feel-good endorphins in your body). You can also help low mood by getting 20 minutes of daylight, especially in winter, to raise serotonin and dopamine levels.

## Mindfulness and meditation

Also, as we saw earlier, simple meditation can create a big difference. Just sitting in a quiet place, for 15 minutes a day, closing your eyes and thinking 'rising' as you breathe in and 'falling' as you breathe out can work wonders. I do this every day, and before writing, and function noticeably better as a consequence. You can increase the alpha brain waves (also known as gamma waves) and slow down your breathing.

As we saw in Chapter 7, recent research was done on the brain of Matthieu Ricard, the famous French Buddhist monk (and self-confessed lab 'guinea pig'), who used to be a neuroscientist before heading for the Himalayas. He has meditated regularly for 35 years and his brain has actually become more developed in the pre-frontal regions, including those areas in the brain controlling compassion and calmness.

The scientist Richard Davidson developed experiments that involved putting Matthieu Ricard into a huge MRI scanner at the Madison Laboratory in the United States. He found that the monk's brain was quite different from other non-meditators. Davidson compared the brains of novice meditators with that of Ricard and other long-term meditating monks, and found some amazing results. The monks who had meditated the longest (in terms of years) had the highest levels of gamma waves. Richard Davidson also found that:

**"**meditation not only changes the workings of the brain in the short-term, but also quite possibly produces permanent changes ... the fact that monks with the most hours of meditation showed the greatest brain changes gives us confidence that the changes are actually produced by mental training**"**

Ricard, *Happiness*, p. 192

So it is possible to train the brain to act differently and to bring about physiological change. It is also possible that the kind of training that CBT promotes can bring about a similar change, in terms of moving your mind from a preoccupation with negative outcomes to a constant focus on positive thinking.

## The way forward

This book has suggested why you might want to consider changing. It has looked at how you might actually embrace and welcome change, in relation to some specific issues that could be affecting your life: mainly fear, anxiety, depression and anger.

It has also looked at how letting negative patterns of thought and behaviour rule your life can hold you back, pull you down and keep you stuck. I hope you will be inspired to bring about positive change in yourself and your life. I sincerely hope you have been able to take something from this book that might give you some CBT insights and practical tools for getting more out of your life.

## The obstacle is the course

Please be aware that in the process of changing:

- **You may well make mistakes.**

- **You are human and may 'forget'** what you have decided upon.

- **You may fail and fail, and then succeed.**

- **It may take some time for you to get used to the CBT way of thinking and being** – that's fine, too.

- **You might find it hard to stick to things** (well maybe you have in the past, but this time ...).

- **You need to reward yourself** in ways that are health giving and fun – make a sticker chart, book yourself a massage or trip to the seaside, a film night out, a nice piece of chocolate cake or a new CD.

- **You need to not let other people put you off.** Some people will be envious that you are trying to sort things out, and may find pleasure in tripping you up – ignore them. Don't get into debates and battles about what you are doing. It's your project and you have every right to try to make your life better for yourself with this tried and tested method.

- **You might find some benefit in asking your GP to refer you** for CBT on the NHS or to pay for an introduction to CBT. There is also online CBT help – so keep yourself motivated any way you need to.

- **You need constantly to begin again.** You can try again, every morning, to start again. Nobody said it would be easy – it won't be. But to give up at the first hurdle is to not give yourself a chance, or the help that you deserve.

- **You'll need to go back through the book regularly**, highlighting the bits that made sense to you; put PostIt notes on the bits that helped. Put stickers on the fridge, on the kettle or computer, in your diary or Blackberry. Keep yourself going, keep travelling forward, keep moving on up: you'll get there in the end.

- **The obstacle is the path** – and you may trip up many times in the days, weeks, months to come, but in the end not doing something to change your life is to give in to inertia, and the downward forces of negative thinking.

Professor Richard Layard of the London School of Economics, and author of *Happiness: Lessons from a New Science* (Penguin, Harmondsworth, 2005) (and a friend of Matthieu Ricard), is the man largely responsible for persuading the UK government to train up 10,000 CBT therapists to help people move forward positively in the UK. He notes:

**❝**you cannot be happy without a wider goal than yourself, but you cannot be happy either without self-knowledge and self-acceptance. If you feel low, there are centuries old philosophies to help ... so happiness comes from the outside and from within. The two are not in contradiction. The true pilgrim fights the evils in the world out there and cultivates the spirit within.**❞**

I think he just might be on to something, don't you?

---

### Your CBT change toolkit

With your CBT toolkit for life you can:

Tool no. 1: Make and stick with your decision to change.

Tool no. 2: Understand how you interpret the world and how you 'tick'.

Tool no. 3: Notice and note down negative thoughts.

Tool no. 4: Track down and eliminate your thinking errors.

Tool no. 5: Clarify problems and conduct experiments.

Tool no. 6: Review your decision, and keep deciding to change.

Tool no. 7: Conquer your anxiety, phobias, trauma, obsessions and addictions.

Tool no. 8: Chase away your 'little black rain cloud'.

Tool no. 9: Slay the dragon and channel your anger.

**Tool no. 10: Boost your confidence and self-esteem.**

---

# The Bestselling Book on Cognitive Behavioural Therapy

Dr Stephen Briers

**brilliant**

**Cognitive Behavioural Therapy**

9780273724902

With plenty of exercises to help you put the theory into practice, this book reveals stories from people just like you, who have used CBT to turn their lives around.

### Brilliant Outcomes

✓ Understand what CBT is, it's methods and models
✓ Put CBT to work to improve your mind and your life
✓ Build practical, step-by-step strategies for tackling any problem

## Get Ready to Shine